World Wis

The Library of Perenn

The Library of Perennial Philosophy is dedicated to the exposition of the timeless Truth underlying the diverse religions. This Truth, often referred to as the *Sophia Perennis*—or Perennial Wisdom—finds its expression in the revealed Scriptures as well as the writings of the great sages and the artistic creations of the traditional worlds.

The Perennial Philosophy provides the intellectual principles capable of explaining both the formal contradictions and the underlying unity of the great religions.

Ranging from the writings of the great sages who have expressed the *Sophia Perennis* in the past, to the perennialist authors of our time, each series of our Library has a different focus. As a whole, they express the inner unanimity, transforming radiance, and irreplaceable values of the great spiritual traditions.

The Universal Spirit of Islam: From the Koran and Hadith appears as one of our selections in the Sacred Worlds series.

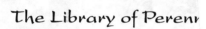

Sacred Worlds Series

The Sacred Worlds series blends images of visual beauty with focused selections from the writings of the great religions of the world, including both Scripture and the writings of the sages and saints. Books in the Sacred Worlds series may be based upon a particular religious tradition, or a theme of interest, such as prayer and virtue, which are found in all manifestations of the sacred.

Other Books by Judith and Michael Oren Fitzgerald

Christian Spirit, World Wisdom, 2004
The Sermon of All Creation: Christians on Nature, World Wisdom, 2005
The Spirit of Indian Women, World Wisdom, 2005
Indian Spirit: Revised & Enlarged, World Wisdom, forthcoming 2006

Other Books by Michael Oren Fitzgerald

Yellowtail: Crow Medicine Man and Sun Dance Chief, University of Oklahoma
     Press, 1991
Light on the Indian World: The Essential Writings of Charles Eastman (Ohiyesa),
     World Wisdom, 2002
Indian Spirit, World Wisdom, 2003
The Foundations of Christian Art: Illustrated, by Titus Burckhardt, edited by
     Michael Oren Fitzgerald, World Wisdom, 2006
Native Spirit: The Sun Dance Way, World Wisdom, 2006
Introduction to Hindu Dharma: By the 68th Jagadguru of Kanchi: Illustrated
     World Wisdom, forthcoming 2007

Films Produced by Michael Oren Fitzgerald

Native Spirit: The Sun Dance Way, World Wisdom, 2007

The Universal Spirit Of Islam:

From the Koran and Hadith

Introduction by

Feisal Abdul Rauf

Edited by

Judith Fitzgerald
and
Michael Oren Fitzgerald

www.worldwisdom.com

The Universal Spirit of Islam:
From the Koran and Hadith
© 2006 World Wisdom, Inc.

Design by Judith Fitzgerald

Cover reference: Mosaic Door, Royal Palace, Casablanca

Library of Congress Cataloging-in-Publication Data

The universal spirit of Islam : from the Koran and Hadith / edited by Judith Fitzgerald and
Michael Oren Fitzgerald ; introduction by Feisal Abdul Rauf.
    p. cm. – (Sacred worlds series)
  Includes bibliographical references.
  ISBN-13: 978-1-933316-16-1 (pbk. : alk. paper)
  ISBN-10: 1-933316-16-0 (pbk. : alk. paper) 1. Islam–Universality. 2. Islam–Appreciation. 3.
Islam–Essence, genius, nature. I. Fitzgerald, Judith, 1951- II. Fitzgerald, Michael Oren, 1949-
III. Series.
  BP170.8.U55 2006
  297.2'8–dc22

                                    2006003805

Printed on acid-free paper in China.

For information address World Wisdom, Inc.
P.O. Box 2682, Bloomington, Indiana 47402-2682

www.worldwisdom.com

CONTENTS

EDITOR'S PREFACE

Can the two primary sources for Islam—the Koran and Hadith —provide us with keys to improve interfaith understanding?

Can we gain a deeper insight into Islam itself through a focused examination of what Islam says about other religions?

This book attempts to answer these questions by presenting quotations from the Koran and Hadith[1] that focus on religions other than Islam.

For each of the world's 1.2 billion Muslims the Koran is the compilation of the Word of God exactly as It was revealed to the Prophet Muhammad[2] over the course of many years. The collection called Hadith is made up of thousands of recorded sayings of Muhammad speaking under various levels of inspiration from God. In this book we only use quotations from the most widely used translations of the Koran[3] and the most widely accepted tradition-al compilations of Hadith.[4] We believe that these sources present traditional Islam in its most authentic form available in the English language.

As our primary focus is on illuminating keys to interfaith dialogue, the great majority of our selections refer to religions other than Islam. These

---

[1] The word *hadith* in Arabic refers to a single utterance or saying of the Prophet. The plural is *ahadith*. We will use the singular "hadith" in all cases, which is now an accepted term in the English language, because the plural will undoubtedly confuse too many readers. When used with the uppercase "H" (i.e. "Hadith"), we are referring to the formal collection of the many individual prophetic utterances.

[2] It is customary to show respect to the Prophet Muhammad by always following a reference to him with one of several Arabic phrases that loosely translated mean "Peace and blessings be upon him." We are not adhering to this convention solely because of the context within which this book appears, not because of any lack of respect.

[3] Our two most frequently used translations are by Marmaduke Pickthall and Yusuf Ali. We have also consulted the translations by Shakir and A.J. Arberry and occasionally substituted one of their formulations or added a parenthesis with an alternative formulation to add clarity. Even with this process it is impossible to convey the multiple levels of meaning that are inherent in the revealed Arabic text.

[4] The death of the Prophet Muhammad in 632 A.D. started a three-hundred year process of col-lecting and archiving all of his sayings and actions. Great care was taken to authenticate each say-ing by tracing it back to Muhammad through an unbroken chain of valid interlocutors (*isnad*). The chain of transmission is usually recounted together with the text (*matn*) of each hadith to

selections are diverse because the Koran names twenty-four different messengers from God who came before Muhammad, and it makes numerous references to additional messengers. For example:

> Verily We have sent messengers before thee (Muhammad); of them there are some whose story We have related to thee, and some whose story We have not related to thee (Koran 40:78).

This hadith is more specific:

> God's Messenger was asked the number which made up the full complement of the prophets, and he replied, "There have been one hundred and twenty-four thousand prophets, among whom were three hundred and fifteen messengers."[5]

To organize these diverse citations we have created seven major sections based upon how each quotation refers to the revelations of non-Islamic religious traditions. The major sections start with "References to Multiple Religions." The other major sections of the book are: "Ancient Messengers from God," "The Abrahamic Tradition," "Judaism," "Christianity," "'People of the Book,'" and "Islam—Universal Truths from the Koran." Within each major section we have identified sub-sections, most of which identify specific messengers or prophets. We first present quotations from the Koran and then we present the Hadith.[6]

The first major section, "References to Multiple Religions," contains sub-sections entitled "General," "The Last Days," and "The Day of Judgment, Paradise, and Hell." Readers familiar with Biblical prophecies will recognize

---

allow the reader to judge its degree of authenticity. A fourteenth century collection entitled the *Mishkat Al-Masabih* contains the six compilations of hadith that are almost universally considered as canonical. To insure authenticity, all of our selections come from the 5,945 hadith contained in the *Mishkat Al-Masabih*, but for easy readability we have chosen not to present the corresponding list of interlocutors and compilers that always begins each hadith.

[5] In the Arabic language, a prophet (*nabi*) is a person inspired by God to bring a warning. A divine messenger (*rasul*) promulgates a new sacred law, which often results in a new religion. Not every prophet is a messenger, but every messenger is by implication a prophet. The Koran also addresses "those who are sent" (*mursaleen*), which refers to both the prophets and the messengers sent by God. The Glossary contains a list of the *mursaleen* who are mentioned by name in the Koran.

various parallels between the Christian and Islamic prophecies regarding the Day of Judgment and the earthly chaos in the last days that will precede it— Armageddon. Many of our citations on this subject reference multiple prophets, but some of these hadith only reference one other prophet. For example, several hadith refer to the anti-Christ, who will appear in the last days before the end of time, and the descent of Jesus, son of Mary, who will prevail over the anti-Christ. Rather than separate these quotations based upon the way they refer to other revelations, they are consolidated in these sub-sections.

The section entitled "Ancient Messengers from God" has sub-sections describing the missions of the Biblical messengers Adam and Noah, in addition to sub-sections that present the lives and work of three other messengers who came before Abraham.

There are more references in the Koran and Hadith to Judaism than there are to Christianity. The section on "Judaism" contains both familiar stories and new information about Jewish messengers. This hadith illustrates the respect given by the Prophet Muhammad to Jewish observances:

> God's Messenger (Muhammad) came to Medina and found the Jews observing the fast on the day of Ashura, so he asked them what was the significance of that day. They replied, "It is a great day on which God delivered Moses and his people and drowned Pharaoh and his people; so Moses observed it as a fast out of gratitude, and we do so also." The Prophet said, "We have as close a connection with Moses as you have," so God's Messenger observed it as a fast himself and gave orders that it should be observed.

As Christianity and Islam are the two largest religions in the world,[7] it is worth noting the many fundamental tenets of Christianity that are shared and accepted by the Koran and Hadith:

---

[6] As we began to review and organize the material we assembled, it became apparent that we had identified a sufficient amount of material for two books. We therefore plan to publish a companion volume limited to Hadith and entitled, *The Spirit of Muhammad: From Hadith* (forthcoming, 2007). Whereas the primary purpose of this book is to present Islam's understanding of religions other than itself, the primary focus of the companion volume will be to present the original revelation of Islam from the words of its messenger that are not included in the Koran.

[7] Statistics on the number of people adhering to each religion are inherently problematic because it is impossible to judge the extent to which a person is practicing a religion. Based upon

- The Virgin Birth of Jesus, conceived by the Holy Spirit;
- Jesus and Mary are the only two people in all creation not touched by Satan at birth;
- The Virgin Mary was chaste, a perfect woman, and chosen above all other women;
- Numerous miracles and inspired teachings by Jesus;
- The resurrection of Jesus after his crucifixion;[8]
- The descent of Jesus to fight the anti-Christ in Armageddon.

Despite various distinctions, the shared beliefs about Christianity greatly outweigh the differences.[9]

To understand how Islam views Christianity and how Islam views Judaism we must start with an understanding of their common lineage. The section entitled "People of the Book"[10] contains various passages that highlight the common spiritual ancestry of Islam, Judaism, and Christianity, which are all traced back to the Abrahamic tradition.

The Koran and Hadith are not without their criticism of Christians and Jews, primarily that many so-called Christians or Jews have strayed from their original faith; however, the Prophet Muhammad also predicted that in time Muslims would lose knowledge of their true faith, as have all preceding civilizations. This saying of Muhammad is one of many such examples:

---

the number of people who have a primary personal faith, Christianity is the largest religion with 33% of the earth's population and Islam is second at 22% of the earth's population. Islam is, by most accounts, the world's fastest growing religion, and its pace of growth (2.9% per year) exceeds the world's population growth (2.3% per year).

[8] This is the most evident meaning of the Koran 4:156-159: "But [the Jews] killed not [the Messiah Jesus], nor crucified him, but so it was made to appear to them; ... for of a surety they killed him not. Nay, God raised him up unto Himself." The resurrection of the Messiah Jesus is also confirmed in this Koranic passage: "(And remember) when God said, 'O Jesus! Verily I am gathering thee and causing thee to ascend unto Me'" (Koran 3:55). Many Muslim theologians do not accept the most straightforward interpretation of these passages and postulate alternative interpretations. The entire verse is presented in the text and this issue is discussed in more detail in the endnotes.

[9] The Koran and Hadith put forward two specific exaggerations by Christians from the Islamic point of view: the requirement of celibacy in the priesthood and the idea that God is one of three equal partners in the "Trinity" of the Father, Son, and Holy Spirit. These criticisms are presented in the text and discussed at more length in the endnotes.

[10] The phrase "People of the Book" refers to the fact that each of these religions possesses a re-

The Prophet said, "There will come a time when knowledge will depart." A man asked him, "How can knowledge depart when we recite the Koran and teach it to our children and they will teach it to their children up until the day of resurrection?" The Prophet replied, "I am astonished at you. I thought you were a man of great learning. Do not these Jews and Christians read the Torah and the *Injil* (the Gospel) without knowing a thing about their contents?"

There are many other hadith that describe how Muslims would fall away from their religion in later days, including a lengthy section of hadith on the trials of the last days (*fitan*) when all men will fall away from religion.[11] These hadith help us recognize that every form of religious faith is under pressure from today's secular, technological society to compromise its fundamental beliefs and turn away from prayer, which eventually leads to an abandonment of faith in God.[12] Perhaps the greatest common ground among the religions is the need to come together to withstand this attack of secularism on every form of spirituality.

The last section, entitled, "Islam—Universal Truths from the Koran," clearly demonstrates the inner unanimity of all religions by identifying many of the universal truths in Islam. Interfaith understanding starts with the recognition that the same all-powerful and all-merciful God created us all and created every great religion.

Many Koranic verses address the same subject from different points of view, thus reinforcing the overall message by repetition. To avoid a disproportionate repetition of similar verses, we have provided an appendix of relevant Koranic verses that we did not utilize.[13] However, this repetition demonstrates that the message contained in these selections is the rule, not the exception. A person with a narrow religious perspective can attempt to disregard the ap-

---

vealed scripture: the Torah, the Gospels, and the Koran.

[11] The great majority of such hadith do not make references to other religions, so they have not been included in this book. The companion book, *The Spirit of Muhammad: From Hadith*, will present a selection of passages to illustrate that Muslims will eventually fall away from their religion.

[12] There are 30 million people in the United States who openly acknowledge they have no religious faith, a number which has grown at more than 5% per year over the past fourteen years.

[13] This Appendix is only a partial list of the most analogous passages and is not a comprehensive concordance that lists all references to religions other than Islam. It provides a starting point to locate additional primary references.

parent meaning of one or another of these quotations, but we believe that the cumulative weight of this authority presents a clear picture of the universal spirit of Islam that is difficult to dismiss.

Islam presents many different faces to the West. It is well beyond our scope to examine the wide spectrum of beliefs that fit under the over-arching umbrella of Islam, including what is often termed traditional Islam, or fundamentalist Islam, or terrorist Islam.[14] This book collects passages that demonstrate how the earliest and incontestable sources of Islamic scripture view other religions, thus providing an unbiased picture before centuries of political conflicts and theological embellishments confused the issue. These quotations allow Muslims and non-Muslims to set aside all preconceptions and examine what authentic Islam actually says about Christianity and Judaism, indeed all other religions.

We first read the Koran and Hadith more than thirty years ago, so when we began our research we knew we would find numerous references to other religions. However, we were quite surprised when we saw the citations collected in one place and organized by subject: the sheer magnitude and precision of the quotations exceeded our expectations. Anyone who has read the Koran or Hadith has seen various references to religions other than Islam, but the impact of seeing many of the most important references together in one place creates a deeper and more lasting impact. We opine that many Muslims will share our surprise, in varying degrees, when they see these excerpts from diverse chapters and volumes together in one place.[15] Any Muslim who believes that Islam is the best religion for everyone in the world—or that other religions are inherently inferior to Islam—needs to ponder the weight of this irrefutable authority.

---

[14] The difficulty of creating and applying inaccurate labels is one of several problems that are examined in detail in Feisal Abdul Rauf's book, entitled *What's Right With Islam* (Harper-San Francisco, 2004). The concept of *jihad*, or holy war, is another such impediment. Reza Shah-Kazemi's article, entitled "Recollecting the Spirit of *Jihad*" in *Islam, Fundamentalism, and the Betrayal of Tradition*, ed. Joseph E.B. Lumbard (World Wisdom, 2004) examines this problem in detail.

[15] Their surprise will increase if they read the many similar verses that are referenced in the Appendix.

These teachings also allow non-Muslims to realize that their fundamental religious beliefs are not in opposition with Islam, but rather share the same universal truths. They also reinforce the fact that all people throughout history are equally susceptible to the danger of losing their real knowledge of their religion. And they demonstrate that God will be the ultimate judge of the outward differences in the religions.

Each traditional civilization that surrounds and supports a major world religion is permeated with inspired beauty in its art, architecture, and crafts—each with its own distinct perfume. We believe the beauty of these traditional worlds is one of the many proofs of the authenticity of their underlying spirituality. Different geographic regions present interesting variations within the basic artistic principles and forms of the respective religions. We have attempted to present sacred art, architecture, and crafts from throughout the Islamic world, including many photographs we have taken during our travels.[16] Plato remarked, "Beauty is the splendor of the true." In this spirit, we believe that the beauty of the photographs complements the Truth contained in the quotations.

We hope the deep respect for other religions that is evident in the Koran and Hadith will imprint itself in the heart of every Muslim. We hope non-Muslims will allow authentic Islam to take its rightful place as one of the world's great religions. We hope that people of all faiths will build a stronger foundation of shared principles that will facilitate interfaith dialogue, starting with recognition of the transcendent unity of religions. If people of diverse faiths

---

[16] Many of the photographs come from our travels to Egypt, India, Iran, Jordan, Malaysia, Mali, Morocco, Niger, Syria, Turkey, and Xinjiang, China.

stand united upon common spiritual truths, then we can better withstand the assault on all spiritual beliefs by today's increasingly secular world. In the process we will also learn something about what is sacred in other faiths and gain a deeper appreciation of what our respective faiths require of us. Above all, we hope that these pages will intensify each person's own life of prayer—because finding a way to come closer to God is the essential message of every religion.

Judith and Michael Fitzgerald
Bloomington, Indiana
October, 2005

INTRODUCTION

Theoretical development in the physical sciences involves identifying universal patterns within local situations and representing them in a language appropriate to each locality; in so doing it thus preserves and respects locality while discerning universality.

The Koranic theme of right religion is this very theme: namely that God the almighty Creator has repeatedly revealed His religion, essential and unique in its universal principles, through many prophet-messengers who have lived in different times, climes, languages, and cultures.[1] Eternal and universal divine Truth has therefore respected locality by expressing itself in the language and culture of each prophet. The divine Word criticizes human beings for confusing locality with universality, thus effectively splitting God's one religion into many divisions.[2]

Our duty as religious people in the twenty-first century is to recognize the points of unity among different revelations. Muslims, especially, are commanded to this at the very beginning of their sacred Scripture: the opening verses of the second chapter of the Koran—addressed to "those who believe in what has been revealed to you [i.e. the Prophet Muhammad] and in what has been revealed before you [i.e. the previous revelations God sent to humankind]"—clearly mandates Muslims to acknowledge that what has been revealed to Muhammad is one in substance, although differing in details and context, with all prior revelations.

By juxtaposing those passages depicting what the Koran says regarding different revelations—especially the Abrahamic faith traditions of Judaism and Christianity—this book not only reveals the common bond of these three faith traditions, but it also urges the reader to examine and probe the underlying transcendent unity of faith itself.

---

[1] Koran 30:30-32 read in a loose but semantically accurate translation: "Direct your self towards upright religion, in accordance with that inner nature that God fashioned people after. There is no altering God's creation: that is what right religion is, but most people don't know that. Turn to Him, keep your godly duty, maintain the prayer, and don't be of those who associate [any other thing or being with God]."

[2] Koran 6:159 reads: "As for those who split up their religion and became sects, you have nothing to do with them. Their issue shall be taken up by God, Who will then apprise them of what they did."

Why is this important? Partly because so much misconception exists as to the relationship between Islam on the one hand, and Judaism and Christianity on the other; and partly because there is the deeper message that the almighty Creator of the universe wants us to heed a message that human beings seem to have such a hard time "getting."

This defines the over-arching objective of interfaith and intrafaith work, the recognition that the phenomenal, philosophical, and psychological differences dividing adherents of different religions are quite similar to those that divide adherents of different sects within one religion. Intrareligious sectarian differences do in fact map interreligious differences.

In a world in which believers in the same religion have difficulty agreeing upon common principles and forms, it is often difficult for adherents of different religions to find common ground. At the risk of simplification, there are three basic positions from which to enter into interfaith dialogue:

- There is no God; or
- God exists but He has only revealed one valid religion; or
- God exists and He has revealed each of the world's major religions.

Interfaith understanding with people who have no belief in God is problematic and almost always non-productive. To a great extent, these religious skeptics have replaced their faith in God with a faith in science.[3] Many observe the apparently irreconcilable differences in the forms of the world's great religions and opine that the major religions are in fundamental disagreement, in which case they must all be wrong. Others point out that a merciful God would not have created just one form of worship and thus forsaken the vast majority of people in the history of the world. These skeptics conclude, for one reason or another, that no religion is valid. It is almost impossible to find common ground to discuss differences in religious points of view if some of the interlocutors think that all religions are false.

---

[3] Scientism is based upon the assumption that rational thought and experimental methods are the means of human knowledge, and that the key to society's well-being is the quantifiable understanding of our material universe. While scientism has produced many important inventions and theories about how the cosmos was created, no scientific method or measurement can explain the most basic question: what is the meaning of life?

A dialogue in which some participants believe that their religion is either the only valid religion, or is the best religion for everyone on earth, breeds skepticism and is hardly conducive to meaningful interfaith dialogue. These points of view frequently lead to proselytism, which is a source of great conflict between the different religions. Even in more favorable situations, such participants almost invariably view anyone of a different faith as inferior. This is a common situation because it is inevitable that most believers should think of their own religion as the best religion—for them it *is* the best religion. The tendency to exaggeration is understandable given that every revelation carries a proclamation to its recipients to believe in this revelation, to proclaim it to unbelievers, and to "shun other false gods." Not every revelation, however, is as explicit in stating that other prophets have brought the same message to other peoples in other times, as is evidenced in these quotations:

> And verily We (God) have raised among every nation a messenger, (with the command), "Serve God and shun false gods" (Koran 16:36).

> Say ye (O believers): "We believe in God, and in the revelation given to us and that which was revealed to Abraham, Ishmael, Isaac, Jacob, and the Tribes, and that (revelation) given to Moses and Jesus and in that (revelation) given to (all) prophets from their Lord. We make no distinction between one and another of them, and unto Him we have surrendered" (Koran 2:136).[4]

We believe true interfaith understanding must be based upon recognizing the existence of one, all-powerful God, who is so merciful that He has manifested Himself in many forms for different collectivities at different times. Thus, there is one timeless Truth underlying the diverse religions—what Frithjof Schuon termed the "transcendent unity of religions."[5] This timeless Truth, often referred to as the *Sophia Perennis* or perennial Wisdom, finds

---

[4] This verse, 2:136, is virtually identical to verse 3:84. The first verse is addressed to all believers and the second verse is addressed to Muhammad. The Arabic is slightly different in use of prepositions, but it is almost impossible to convey that fine a difference in English.

[5] The late Swiss philosopher Frithjof Schuon (1907-1998) wrote nearly thirty books on spirituality. He is the preeminent author of the Perennialist School of thought, which emerged at the beginning of the twentieth century. Schuon's writings illuminate the inner meaning contained within the sacred writings of each religion—its "esoteric" aspect.

its expression in the revealed Scriptures, as well as in the oral and written words of the great spiritual masters, and in the artistic creations of the traditional worlds. A comparative study of the canonical writings of the different religions, especially revealed Scripture, is therefore an indispensable key to interfaith understanding. Several principles can provide important context for a comparative study.

First, it is evident that every revelation is addressed to a specific people in a specific historical circumstance. For example, the Prophet of Islam was charged with leading a pagan people of the Arabian Peninsula, who were in a state of spiritual and moral decadence, back to the pristine monotheism of Adam and Abraham. However, if there is a transcendent unity of religions, then there must also be shared universal truths within each religion that are addressed to all humanity. For example, the Koran and Hadith sometimes limit their messages to the Arabs of Muhammad's time and culture; yet, in other instances, they address the "children of Adam"—humankind as such—and appeal to that which is common to all people. We can also think of these as the historical and the supra-historical teachings of the Scriptures. This book demonstrates that Islam has a deep appreciation of supra-historical manifestations of the Divine outside of the world of seventh century Arabia.

In addition to these identifiable universal truths, the sacred Scriptures and writings of the great sages of each of the major religions have different levels of meaning that may not be apparent to each and every believer. Islam refers to an outward or revealed aspect (*zahir*), and an inner, hidden one (*batin*). The following hadith reinforce this principle and provide practical advice to believers when the meaning of Scripture is not clear:

> The Koran came down showing five aspects: what is permissible, what is prohibited, what is firmly fixed, what is obscure, and parables. So treat what is permissible as permissible and what is prohibited as prohibited, act upon what is firmly fixed, believe in what is obscure, and take a lesson from the parables.

> Things are of three categories: a matter whose right guidance is clear, which you must follow; a matter whose error is clear, which you must avoid; and a matter about which there is a difference of opinion, which you must entrust to God.

By analogy, we should not be troubled if the reasons for the apparently irreconcilable differences in the forms of the religions appear ambiguous. This happens because the differences involve various levels of meaning at varying levels of essential universality or incidental locality. If we consider that the identifiable shared universal truths represent essential Truth, then the conflicting forms of the religions are based upon certain principles that have a more relative importance. A principle of relative importance may not be necessary for all people, but it may be of compelling importance for a particular people based upon their collective temperament. Muhammad has two sayings that support the idea that different people have different tendencies and each religion has a different character or signature:

Every people has a temptation, and my people's temptation is property.

Every religion has a signature, and the signature of Islam is modesty.

This book highlights certain common themes underlining the proposition that while (authentic) religions may look different, they all come from the same Source.[6] When people see the night sky from different parts of the earth, or at different times of the year from the same location, their descriptions will vary even though it is the self-same universe. Is it any wonder that the same all-merciful God Who created the breathtaking wonders of our universe, has revealed different manifestations of His Truth to different peoples over the millennia?

Interfaith dialogue, therefore, does not mean that the outward laws of religion may be disregarded—quite the contrary. Every religion states that it is not possible to create a new religion by combining elements from different forms of spirituality—religion and spirituality must be on God's terms, not on man's terms. Rather, the integral foundation for interfaith dialogue is based upon the realization that:

- The universal truths within the diverse religions are identical;
- Outward differences in the forms of the religions do not alter their inner unanimity;

---

[6] An examination of the Divine logic underlying the apparent contradictions in the forms of the diverse religions is outside the scope of this introduction.

- Each religion is providential for the people and time in which it has been revealed;
- No revealed religion or messenger of God can be fundamentally superior to another;
- There are different levels and signatures to each revelation that collectively describe the Divine plan;
- Each person's primary responsibility is to his or her personal relationship to God, trusting that He will judge our differences.

The following selection of Koranic passages and hadith support these propositions:

To those who believe in God and His messengers and make no distinction between any of the messengers, We shall soon give their (due) rewards, for God is oft-forgiving, most merciful (4:152).

And unto thee have We revealed the Book (Koran) with the Truth, confirming whatever Scripture was before it.... For each (people) We have appointed a divine law and a traced-out way. Had God willed He could have made you one community (5:48).

We did send messengers before thee.... For each period is a Scripture (revealed) (13:38).

We never sent a messenger except (to teach) in the language of his (own) people, in order to make (the message) clear to them (14:4).

To every people have We appointed (different) rites and ceremonies which they must follow, so let them not then dispute with thee on the matter; but do thou invite (them) to thy Lord, for thou art assuredly on the right way. And if they wrangle with thee, say, "God is best aware of what ye do." God will judge between you on the Day of Resurrection concerning that wherein ye used to differ (22:67-69).

Nothing is said to thee that was not said to the messengers before thee (41:43).

INTRODUCTION

When the prophet Muhammad heard someone say that he was superior to the prophet Jonah, he said, "Do not say that I am better than Jonah. Do not treat some of the prophets of God as superior to others."

O ye messengers ... verily this your religion (community) is one religion (community) and I am your Lord, so keep your duty unto Me (23:52).

This last quotation contains an important declaration for every believer, regardless of faith—focus on your individual duty to God, not upon outward differences in the forms of worship.

These quotations are not just messages directed to followers of the message of Muhammad; they are universal truths from the Koran—addressed to all of humanity. These inspirational selections present the same essential spiritual truths that are found within each of the world's major religions, offered in the hope that they will compel people who have lost their faith in God to reconsider; to stimulate adherents of other faiths to recognize their common bond with Muslims; and to contribute to a deepening of the life of prayer for practicing Muslims, and, indeed, for people of all faiths.

Imam Feisal Abdul Rauf
New York, 2005

"The world is but an hour, so spend it doing pious things." Ali

References to Multiple Religions

General
The Last Days
The Day of Judgment, Paradise, and Hell

 General

And verily We gave unto Moses the Scripture and We caused a train of messengers to follow after him, and We gave unto Jesus, son of Mary, clear proofs (of God's sovereignty), and We supported him with the holy Spirit. Is it ever so, that, when there cometh unto you a messenger (from God) with that which ye yourselves desire not, ye grow arrogant, and some ye disbelieve and some ye slay?
2: 87

Say ye (O believers): "We believe in God, and in the revelation given to us and that which was revealed to Abraham, Ishmael, Isaac, Jacob, and the Tribes, and that (revelation) given to Moses and Jesus and in that (revelation) given to (all) prophets from their Lord. We make no distinction between one and another of them, and unto Him we have surrendered."
2: 136

Righteous is he who believeth in God and the Last Day and the angels and the Scripture and the prophets; and (who) giveth wealth, for love of Him, to kinsfolk and to orphans and the needy and the wayfarer and to those who ask, and to set slaves free; and (who) observeth proper worship and payeth the poor-due; and those who keep their treaty when they make one; and the patient in tribulation and adversity and time of stress. Such are they who are sincere; such are the God-fearing.
2: 177

Mankind were one community, and God sent (unto them) prophets as bearers of good tidings and as warners, and revealed therewith the Scripture with the Truth that it might judge between mankind concerning that wherein they differed. And those unto whom (the Scripture) was given differed concerning it, after clear proofs had come unto them, through hatred one of another. And God by His will guided those who believe unto the truth of that concerning which they differed. God guideth whom He will unto a straight path.
2: 213

Al-Hakin Mosque
Isfahan, Iran

God did choose Adam and Noah, the family of Abraham, and the family of Imran (the father of the Virgin Mary) above all people.
3: 33

No prophet could (ever) be false to his trust.
3: 161

It is not (the purpose) of God to leave you in your present state until He shall separate the wicked from the good, and it is not (the purpose of) God to let you know the unseen; but God chooseth of His messengers whom He will, (to receive knowledge thereof), so believe in God and His messengers. If ye believe and ward off (evil), yours will be a vast reward.
3: 179

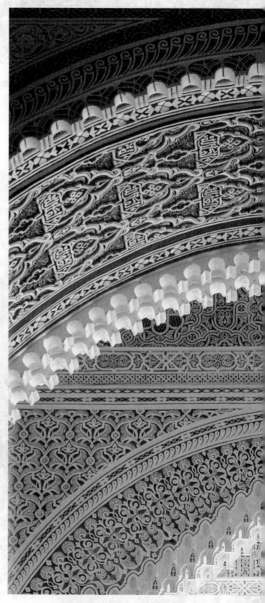

Royal Palace throne room
Rabat, Morocco

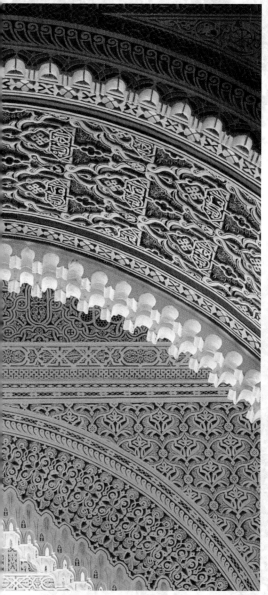

Our Lord! Grant us what Thou didst promise unto us through Thy messengers, and save us from shame on the Day of Judgment, for Thou never breakest Thy promise.
3: 194

But how (will it be with them) when We bring of every people a witness, and We bring thee (O Muhammad) a witness against these (your people)? On that day those who disbelieved and disobeyed their messenger will wish that they were level with the ground, and they can hide no fact from God.
4: 41-42

O ye who believe! Believe in God and His messenger, and the Scripture which He hath sent to His messenger and the Scripture which He sent to those before (him). Any who denieth God, His angels, His Scriptures, His messengers, and the Day of Judgment, hath gone far, far astray.
4: 136

Verily those who disbelieve in God and His messengers, and seek to make distinction between God and His messengers, and say, "We believe in some and disbelieve in others, and seek to choose a way in between," such are disbelievers in truth; and for disbelievers We
[continued]

[continued]

prepare a shameful doom. To those who believe in God and His messengers and make no distinction between any of the messengers, we shall soon give their (due) rewards, for God is oft-forgiving, most merciful.
4: 150-52

Verily We inspire thee as We inspired Noah and the prophets after him, as We inspired Abraham and Ishmael and Isaac and Jacob and the Tribes, and Jesus and Job and Jonah and Aaron and Solomon, and as We imparted unto David the Psalms; and messengers We have mentioned unto thee before and messengers We have not mentioned unto thee; and God spoke directly unto Moses; messengers who gave good news as well as warning, that mankind, after (the coming) of the messengers, should have no plea against God—for God is exalted in power, wise.
4: 163-165

And unto thee have We revealed the Book (Koran) with the truth, confirming whatever Scripture was before it.... For each (people) We have appointed a divine law and a traced-out way. Had God willed He could have made you one community.
5: 48

Rejected were the messengers before thee. With patience and constancy they bore their rejection and their wrongs, until Our aid did reach them— there is none that can alter the words (and decrees) of God. Already hast thou received some of the tidings of those messengers.
6: 34

Before thee We sent (messengers) to many nations, and We afflicted the nations with suffering and adversity, that they might learn humility. When the suffering reached them from Us, why then did they not learn humility? On the contrary their hearts became hardened and Satan made their (sinful) acts seem alluring to them. But when they forgot the warning they had received, We opened to them the gates of all (good) things, until, in the midst of their enjoyment of Our gifts, on a sudden, We called them to account, when verily they were plunged in despair!
6: 42-44

Illuminated Koran
Surah of Mary
Lahore, Pakistan, c. 1573

We gave it (Our message) unto Abraham against his folk. We raise unto degrees of wisdom whom We will, for verily thy Lord is wise, aware. And We bestowed upon him Isaac and Jacob, each of them We guided; and Noah did We guide aforetime; and of his seed (We guided) David and Solomon and Job and Joseph and Moses and Aaron—thus do We reward the good. And Zachariah and John and Jesus and Elias, each one (of them) was of the righteous; and Ishmael and Elisha and Jonah and Lot, each one (of them) did We prefer above (Our) creatures, with some of their forefathers and their offspring and their brethren; and We chose them and guided them unto a straight path. Such is the guidance of God. He giveth that guidance to whom He pleaseth of His worshippers. But if they had set up (for worship) aught beside Him, (all) that they did would have been vain. Those are they unto whom We gave the Scripture and command and prophethood. But if these disbelieve therein, then indeed We shall entrust it to a people who will not be disbelievers therein. Those were the (prophets) who received God's guidance—copy the guidance they received.
6: 84-91

We destroyed the generations before you when they did wrong; and their messengers (from God) came unto them with clear proofs (of His sovereignty) but they would not believe. Thus do We reward the guilty folk.
10: 13

To every people (was sent) a messenger; when their messenger comes (before them on the Day of Judgment), the matter will be judged between them with justice, and they will not be wronged.
10: 47

These are some of the stories of communities which We relate unto thee; of them some are standing, and some have been mown down (by the sickle of time). It was not We that wronged them, they wronged their own souls. The deities, other than God, whom they invoked, profited them no whit when there issued the decree of thy Lord; nor did they add

aught (to their lot) but perdition! Such is the chastisement of thy Lord when He chastises communities in the midst of their wrong; grievous, indeed, and severe is His chastisement. In that is a sign for those who fear the penalty of the hereafter—that is a day for which mankind will be gathered together, that will be a Day of Testimony. Nor shall We delay it but for a term appointed. The day it arrives, no soul shall speak except by His leave; of those (gathered) some will be wretched and some will be blessed. Those who are wretched shall be in the fire. There will be for them therein (nothing but) the heaving of sighs and sobs. And those who are blessed shall be in the garden. They will dwell therein for all the time that the heavens and the earth endure, except as thy Lord willeth, a gift without break.
11: 100-108

All that we relate to thee of the stories of the messengers—with it We make firm thy heart. In them there cometh to thee the Truth, and an exhortation and a message of remembrance to those who believe.
11: 120

Nor did We send before thee (as messengers) any but men, whom we did inspire, (men) living in human habitations. Do they not travel through the earth, and see what was the end of those before them?... There is, in their stories, instruction for men endued with understanding. It is not a tale invented, but a confirmation of what went before it, a detailed exposition of all things, and a guide and a mercy to any such as believe.
12: 109-111

Mocked were (many) messengers before thee, but I granted respite to the unbelievers, and finally I punished them; then how (terrible) was my requital!
13: 32

We did send messengers before thee, and appointed for them wives and children, and it was never the part of a messenger to bring a sign except as God permitted. For each period is a Scripture (revealed).
13: 38

We never sent a messenger except (to teach) in the language of his (own) people, in order to make (the message) clear to them. Then God leaves straying those whom He pleases and guides whom He pleases. He is the mighty, the wise.
14: 4

And verily We have raised among every nation a messenger, (with the command), "Serve God and shun false gods." Then some people (there were) whom God guided, and some of them (there were) upon whom error became inevitably (established). So travel through the earth, and see what was the end of those who denied (the truth).
16: 36

Verily God is Beautiful and He loves Beauty

Who receiveth guidance, receiveth it for his own benefit, and who goeth astray doth so to his own loss. No bearer of burdens can bear the burden of another, nor would We visit them with Our wrath until We had sent a messenger (to give warning). When We decide to destroy a population, We (first) send commandments to those among them who are given the good things of this life and yet transgress; and then the Word (of warning) is proved true against them and We destroy them utterly. How many generations have We destroyed after Noah? It suffices for thy Lord to note and see the sins of His servants. If any do wish for the transitory things (of this life), We readily grant them—such things as We will to such person as We will. In the end have We provided hell for them—they will burn therein, disgraced and rejected. Those who do wish for the (things of) the hereafter, and strive therefore with all due striving, and have faith—they are the ones whose striving is acceptable (to God).
17: 15-19

Those were some of the prophets on whom God did bestow His grace—of the posterity of Adam, and of those whom We carried (in the Ark) with Noah, and of the posterity of Abraham and Israel of those whom

(continued)

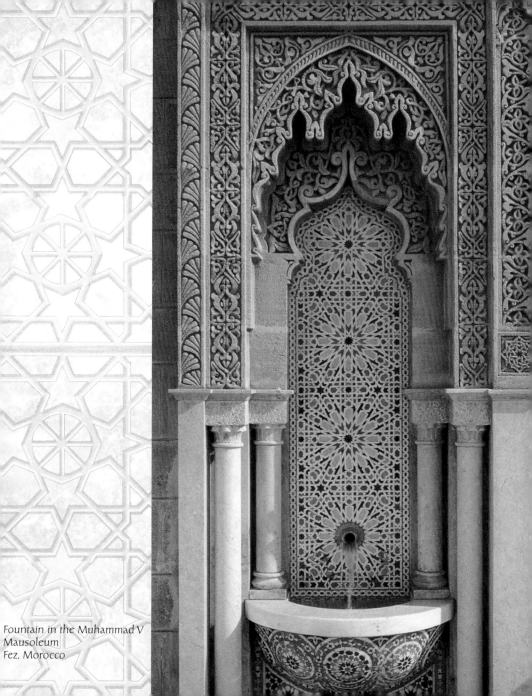

Fountain in the Muhammad V
Mausoleum
Fez, Morocco

[continued]
We guided and chose. Whenever the signs of (God) most gracious were rehearsed to them, they would fall down in prostrate adoration and in tears. But after them there followed a posterity who missed prayers and followed after lusts; soon, then, will they face destruction—except those who repent and believe, and work righteousness, for these will enter the garden and will not be wronged in the least.
19: 58-60

And when Our clear signs are recited unto them, those who disbelieve say unto those who believe, "Which of the two parties (yours or ours) is better in position, and more imposing as an army?" How many a generation have We destroyed before them, who were more imposing in respect of gear and outward seeming! Say, "If any men go astray, (God) most gracious extends (the rope) to them, until, when they see the warning of God (being fulfilled)—either in punishment or in (the approach of) the Hour (of doom)—they will at length realize who is worst in position, and (who) weakest in forces!
19: 73-75

Before thee, also, the messengers We sent were but men, to whom We granted inspiration. If ye realize this not, ask of those who possess the message.... In the end We fulfilled to
[continued]

[continued]

them Our promise, and We saved them and those whom We pleased, but We destroyed those who transgressed beyond bounds.
21: 7-9

We bestowed on Abraham of old his rectitude of conduct, and well were We acquainted with him…. Abraham said, "Your Lord is the Lord of the heavens and the earth, He who created them (from nothing), and I am a witness to this (Truth).".… And We rescued Abraham and (his nephew) Lot (and brought them) to the land which We have blessed for (all) peoples. And We bestowed upon him Isaac, and Jacob as a grandson. Each of them We made righteous. And We made them leaders, guiding (men) by Our command; and We sent them inspiration to do good deeds, to establish regular prayers, and to practice regular charity; and they constantly served Us (alone). And unto Lot we gave judgment and knowledge, and We delivered him from the community that did abominations — verily they were folk of evil, lewd. And We admitted him to Our mercy, for he was one of the righteous. (Remember) Noah, when he cried (to Us) aforetime; We listened to his (prayer) and delivered him and his family from great affliction. And delivered him from the people who denied Our revelations — verily they were folk of evil, therefore did We drown them all.

[continued]

Line from a
North African
Koran, c. 1304

[continued]

And remember David and Solomon, when they gave judgment in the
matter of the field into which the sheep of certain people had strayed
by night, and We did witness their judgment. To Solomon We inspired
the (right) understanding of the matter, and unto each of them We gave
judgment and knowledge. It was Our power that made the hills and the
birds celebrate Our praises along with David—it was We who did (all
these things).
21: 51-79

Verily those who believe (this revelation), and those who are Jews, and
the Sabaeans and the Christians and the Magians and the idolaters—Verily God will decide between them on the Day of Resurrection. Verily God
is witness over all things.
22: 17

To every people have We appointed (different) rites and ceremonies
which they must follow, so let them not then dispute with thee on the
matter; but do thou invite (them) to thy Lord, for thou art assuredly on the
right way. And if they wrangle with thee, say, "God is best aware of what
ye do. God will judge between you on the Day of Resurrection concerning that wherein ye used to differ."
22: 67-69

Then sent We our messengers in succession; every time there came to
a people their messenger, they accused him of falsehood, so We made
them follow each other (in punishment). We made them as a tale (that is
told)—so away with a people that will not believe! [The stories of Moses,
and Jesus and the Virgin Mary are briefly told.] O ye messengers! Enjoy
(all) things good and pure, and work righteousness, for I am well acquainted with (all) that ye do. And verily this your religion is one religion
and I am your Lord, so keep your duty unto Me. But they (mankind) have

[continued]

Prayer niche of Oljaytu
Friday Mosque
Isfahan, Iran

Domed ceiling of the Ayn Sofia
Istanbul, Turkey

[continued]

broken their religion among them into sects, each group rejoicing in its tenets. But leave them in their confused ignorance for a time.
23: 44-54

And how many populations We destroyed, which exulted in their life (of ease and plenty)! Now those habitations of theirs, after them, are deserted—all but a (miserable) few! We are their heirs! Nor was thy Lord the one to destroy a population until He had sent to its center a messenger, rehearsing to them Our signs; nor did We destroy a population except when its members practiced iniquity. The (material) things which ye are given are but the conveniences of this life and the glitter thereof; but that which is with God is better and more enduring; will ye not then be wise?
28: 58-60

We did indeed send, before thee, messengers to their (respective) peoples, and they came to them with clear signs. Then, to those who transgressed, We meted out retribution; and it was due from Us to aid those who believed.
30: 47

It (the Koran) is the Truth from thy Lord, that thou mayest admonish a people to whom no warner has come before thee, in order that they may receive guidance.
32: 3

And when We exacted a covenant from the prophets, and from thee (O Muhammad) and from Noah and Abraham and Moses and Jesus, son of Mary. We took from them a solemn covenant that He may ask the loyal of their loyalty—and He hath prepared a painful doom for the unfaithful.
33: 7-8

Verily We have sent thee in truth, as a bearer of glad tidings, and as a warner; and there never was a people, without a warner having lived among them (in the past). And if they reject thee, so did their predecessors (even though) their messengers came unto them with clear proofs (of God's sovereignty), and with the Psalms and the Scripture giving light. Then seized I those who disbelieved, and how intense was My abhorrence!
35: 24-26

God has revealed (from time to time) the most beautiful message in the form of a Book, consistent with itself, (yet) repeating (its teaching in various aspects). The skins of those who fear their Lord tremble thereat; then their skins and their hearts do soften to the celebration of God's praises.
39: 23

Verily We have sent messengers before thee; of them there are some whose story We have related to thee, and some whose story We have not related to thee. It was not (possible) for any messenger to bring a sign except by the leave of God, but when the command of God was issued, the matter was decided in truth and justice, and there perished, there and then, those who stood on falsehoods.
40: 78

Prayer niche of the Grand Mosque of Cordoba, Cordoba, Spain

Merinid Mosque at Chellah,
Rabat, Morocco

Nothing is said to thee that was not said to the messengers before thee, that thy Lord has at His command (all) forgiveness as well as a most grievous penalty.
41: 43

The same religion has He established for you as that which He enjoined on Noah—which We have sent by inspiration to thee—and that which We enjoined on Abraham, Moses, and Jesus: namely, that ye should remain steadfast in religion, and make no divisions therein. To those who worship other things than God, hard is the (way) to which thou callest them. God chooses to Himself those whom He pleases, and guides to Himself those who turn (to Him).
42: 13

It is not fitting for a man that God should speak to him except by inspiration, or from behind a veil, or by the sending of a messenger to reveal, with God's permission, what God wills, for He is most high, most wise.
42: 51

Just in the same way, whenever We sent a warner before thee (Muhammad) to any people, the wealthy ones among them said, "We found our fathers following a certain religion, and we will certainly follow in their footsteps." (And the warner) said, "What! Even if I brought you better guidance than that which ye found your fathers following?" They said, "For us, we deny that ye (prophets) are sent (on a mission at all)." So We exacted retribution from them. Now see what was the end of those who rejected (truth)!
43: 23-25

Even so there came no messenger unto those before them but they said, "A wizard or a madman!" Have they handed down (the saying) as a legacy one unto another? Nay, they are people transgressing beyond bounds.
51: 52-53

We verily sent Our messengers with clear proofs, and revealed with them the Scripture and the balance, that mankind may observe right measure; and He revealed iron, wherein is mighty power and (many) uses for mankind, and that God may know him who helpeth Him and His messengers, though unseen. Verily God is strong, almighty. And We verily sent Noah and Abraham and placed the prophethood and the Scripture among their seed, and among them there is he who goeth right, but many of them are evil livers. Then We caused Our messengers to follow in their footsteps; and We caused Jesus, son of Mary, to follow, and gave him the Gospel and placed compassion and mercy in the hearts of those who followed him. But monasticism they invented—We ordained it not for them.... So We give those of them who believe their reward, but many of them are evil livers.[1]
57: 25-27

God has decreed, "It is I and My messengers who must prevail," for God is One—full of strength, able to enforce His will.
58: 21

(God is) the knower of the unseen, and He revealeth unto none His secret, save unto every messenger whom He hath chosen.
72: 26-27

The hereafter is better and more enduring. And this is in the books of the earliest (revelations)—the Books of Abraham and Moses.
87: 17-19

One day when we were with God's messenger, a man with very white clothing and very black hair came up to us. No mark of travel was visible on him, and none of us recognized him. Sitting down beside the Prophet, leaning his knees against his, and placing his hands on his thighs, he said, "Tell me, Muhammad, about Islam." The Prophet replied, "Islam means that you should testify that there is no god but God and that Muhammad is God's messenger, that you should observe the prayer (salat), pay the compulsory charity (zakat), fast during Ramadan (the month of compulsory fasting), and make the pilgrimage to the House (Kaaba) if you have the means to go." The stranger said, "You have spoken the truth." We were surprised at his questioning him and then declaring that he spoke the truth. He said, "Now tell me about faith (iman)." The Prophet replied, "It means that you should believe in God, His angels, His Books, His prophets, and the Last Day, and that you should believe in the decreeing both of good and evil." Remarking that he had spoken the truth, he then said, "Now tell me about doing good (ihsan)." The Prophet replied, "It means that you should worship God as though you saw Him, for He sees you though you do not see Him." He said, "Now tell me about the Hour (of the Day of Judgment)." The Prophet replied, "The one who is asked about it is no better informed than the one who is asking." The stranger said, "Then tell me about its signs (preceding the Day of Judgment)." The Prophet replied, "That a maid-servant should beget her mistress, and that you should see barefooted, naked, poor men and shepherds exalting themselves in buildings." The stranger then went away, and after a time the Prophet said, "Do you know who the questioner was? He was Gabriel who came to you to teach you your religion." [2]
hadith

Man praying in a Mosque
India

God's messenger told of Adam and Moses holding a disputation in their Lord's presence and of Adam getting the better of Moses in argument. Moses said, "You are Adam whom God created with His hand, into whom He breathed of His spirit, to whom He made the angels do obeisance, and whom He caused to dwell in His garden; then because of your sin you caused mankind to come down to the earth." Adam replied, "And you are Moses whom God chose to deliver His messages and to address, to whom He gave the tablets on which everything was explained, and whom He brought near as a confidant. How long before I was created did you find that God had written the Torah?" Moses said, "Forty years." Adam asked, "Did you find in it, 'And Adam disobeyed his Lord and erred'?" On being told that he did, he said, "Do you then blame me for doing a deed which God had decreed that I should do forty years before He created me?" God's messenger said, "So Adam got the better of Moses in argument."
hadith

God's messenger came out to a group of Muslims who were arguing about God's decree. He was angry and his face became so red that it looked as if pomegranate seeds had been burst open on his cheeks. He then said, "Is this what you were commanded to do, or was it for this purpose that I was sent to you? Your predecessors perished only when they argued about this matter. I adjure you, I adjure you, not to argue about it."
hadith

No people have gone astray after following right guidance unless they have been led into disputation.
hadith

At the beginning of every century God will send one who will renew its religion for this people. In every successive century those who are reliable authorities will preserve this knowledge, rejecting the changes made by extremists, the plagiarisms of those who make false claims for themselves, and the interpretations of the ignorant.
hadith

The Prophet said, "There will come a time when knowledge will depart." He was asked, "How can knowledge depart when we recite the Koran and teach it to our children and they will teach it to their children up until the Day of Resurrection? The Prophet replied, "I am astonished at you. I thought you were a man of great learning. Do not these Jews and Christians read the Torah and the Gospel without knowing a thing about their contents?"
hadith

When the Prophet was asked which people suffered the greatest affliction he replied, "The prophets, then those who come next to them, then those who come next to them. A man is afflicted in keeping with his religion; if he is firm in his religion his trial is severe, but if there is weakness in his religion it is made light for him, and it continues like that until he walks on the earth firm in his religion."
hadith

"The pilgrimage to Mecca has been ordained for you people, so perform it." A man asked the Prophet whether it should be performed annually, but God's messenger gave no reply until he was asked the question three times. Then the Prophet said, "If I were to say that it should, it would be obligatory and you would not be able to perform it. Leave me alone as long as I have said nothing to you, for your predecessors perished simply on account of their much questioning and their disagreement with their prophets. But when I command you to do anything, obey it as much as you can; and when I forbid you to do anything, leave it alone."
hadith

The best thing which I and the prophets before me have said is, "There is no god but God, alone, who has no partner; to Him belongs the dominion, to Him is praise due, and He is omnipotent."
hadith

The Prophet said, "God has not sent a prophet who did not work as a shepherd." His companions asked whether this was also true of him and he replied, "Yes, I used to be a shepherd for the people of Mecca."
hadith

nd Mosque
epur Sikri, India

When a wealthy woman from a prominent tribe committed a theft, the Prophet was asked if he would intercede for her regarding the punishment prescribed by God. God's messenger got up and gave an address, saying, "What destroyed your predecessors was that when a person of rank among them committed a theft they left him alone, but when a weak one of their number committed a theft they inflicted the prescribed punishment on him. I swear by God that if Fatima, daughter of Muhammad, should steal I would have her hand cut off."
hadith

When the Jews fell into acts of disobedience, their learned men forbade them, but they did not refrain. Their learned men then sat together with them in their gatherings, ate with them and drank with them, and God mingled their hearts with one another and cursed them all by the tongue of David and Jesus, son of Mary. That was because they disobeyed and transgressed. I swear by God, you must enjoin what is reputable, prohibit what is disreputable, prevent the wrongdoer, bend him into conformity with what is right, and restrict him to what is right, or God will mingle your hearts together and curse you as He cursed them.
hadith

Among the prophets there is one who was believed by only one man out of his people.
hadith

The Fountain of the Court of the Lions
Alhambra, Spain

God's messenger was asked the number which made up the full comple-
ment of the prophets, and he replied, "There have been one hundred and
twenty-four thousand prophets, among whom were three hundred and
fifteen messengers."
hadith

God's messenger was asked who was the first of the prophets, and he
replied that it was Adam. He was asked if he (Adam) was really a prophet
and he replied, "Yes, he was a prophet to whom a message was given."
God's messenger was then asked how many messengers there had been,
and he replied, "There have been three hundred and between ten and
twenty in all."
hadith

No prophet has failed to be given a miracle which caused men to believe
in him when it was seen. What I have been given is simply a revelation
which God gave to me, and I hope I may be the one of them who will
have the largest following on the day of resurrection.
hadith

Every people has a temptation, and my people's temptation is property.
hadith

Every religion has a character, and the character of Islam is modesty.
hadith

God's prophet spoke about the night when he was taken up to heaven,
saying, "While I was lying down, someone came to me and made a split
from here to here (meaning from the pit of his chest to the hair below
his navel), then took out my heart. I was next brought a gold dish full of
faith, and my heart was washed, then filled up and put back. I was then
brought a beast smaller than a mule and larger than a donkey, which was
white, was called al-Buraq, and stepped a distance equal to the range of
its vision. I was mounted on it, and Gabriel went with me until he came
to the lowest heaven. He asked that the gate be opened, and when he
was asked who he was, he replied that he was Gabriel. He was asked who
was with him and replied that it was Muhammad. He was asked whether

[continued]

Ascension of the Prophet Muhammad
Persian miniature

33

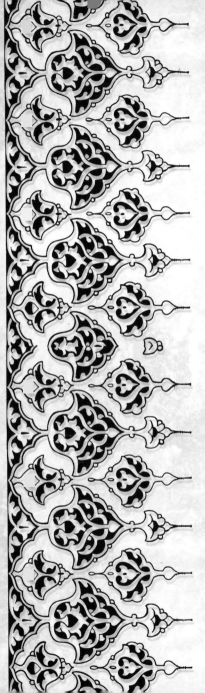

[continued]

he had been sent for, and when he replied that that was so, the words were uttered, 'Welcome; his coming is good,' and the gate was opened. When I entered Adam was there, and Gabriel said, 'This is your father Adam, so give him a salutation.' I did so, and when he had returned my salutation he said, 'Welcome to the good son and the good prophet.' Gabriel then took me up until he came to the second heaven. He asked that the gate be opened, and when he was asked who he was he replied that he was Gabriel. He was asked who was with him and replied that it was Muhammad. He was asked whether he had been sent for, and when he replied that that was so, the words were uttered, 'Welcome; his coming is good,' and the gate was opened. When I entered John and Jesus, who were cousins on the mother's side, were there, and Gabriel said, 'These are John and Jesus, so give them a salutation.' I did so, and when they had returned my salutation they said, 'Welcome to the good brother and the good prophet.' Gabriel then took me up to the third heaven. [The same salutations were repeated] and the gate was opened. When I entered Joseph was there, and Gabriel said, 'This is Joseph, so give him a salutation.' [Similar salutations were repeated.] Gabriel then took me up until he came to the fourth heaven. [The same salutations were repeated] and the gate was opened. When I entered Enoch was there, and Gabriel said, 'This is Enoch, so give him a salutation.' [Similar salutations were repeated.] Gabriel then took me up until he came to the fifth heaven. [The same salutations were repeated] and the gate was opened. When I entered Aaron was there, and

Gabriel said, 'This is Aaron, so give him a salutation.' [Similar salutations were repeated.] Gabriel then took me up until he came to the sixth heaven. [The same salutations were repeated] and the gate was opened. When I entered Moses was there, and Gabriel said, 'This is Moses, so give him a salutation.' [Similar salutations were repeated.] Then when I passed on he wept, and when he was asked what was making him weep he replied, 'I am weeping because more followers of a young man who was commissioned after my time will enter Paradise than of mine.' Gabriel then took me up to the seventh heaven. [The same salutations were repeated] and the gate was opened. When I entered Abraham was there, and Gabriel said, 'This is your father Abraham, so give him a salutation.' I did so, and when he had returned my salutation he said, 'Welcome to the good son and the good prophet.'...

"When what God commands overshadows it, it changes, and none of God's creatures can describe it because of its beauty. God revealed to me what He revealed and made obligatory for me fifty prayers every day and night. I came down to Moses, who asked what my Lord had made obligatory for my people, and when I told him He had prescribed fifty prayers every day and night, he said, 'Go back to your Lord and ask Him to make things lighter, for your people are not capable of that. I have tested and had experience of the Tribes of Israel.' I went back to my Lord and said, 'O my Lord, make things lighter for my people,' so He relieved me of five. When I returned to Moses and told him He had relieved me of five he said, 'Your people are not capable of that, so go back to your Lord and ask Him to make things lighter.' I then kept going back and forth between my Lord and Moses until He said, 'They are five prayers every day and night, Muhammad, each being credited as ten, so that makes fifty times of prayer. He who intends to do a good deed and does not do it will have a good deed recorded for him, and if he does it, it will be recorded for him as ten; whereas he who intends to do an evil and does not do it will have nothing recorded for him, and if he does it one evil deed will be recorded for him.' I then came down, and when I came to Moses and told him, he said, 'Go back to your Lord and ask Him to make things lighter.'" God's messenger said that he replied, "I have gone back to my Lord until I am ashamed to face Him. Now I am satisfied and I submit."
hadith

On another occasion when the Prophet was speaking about his night journey to heaven, he said, "I found Adam who welcomed me and prayed for my well-being." Regarding the third heaven he said, "I found Joseph who had been given half of beauty, and he welcomed me and prayed for my well-being." But he did not mention the weeping of Moses. Regarding the seventh heaven he said, "I found Abraham supporting his back against the frequented house which is entered daily by seventy thousand angels who do not return to it."
hadith

"No prophet becomes ill without being given his choice between this world and the next." During the illness of which he died, God's messenger was afflicted by severe hoarseness and his wife, Aisha, heard him say, "With those of the prophets, upright, martyrs and pious ones to whom Thou hast shown favor," so she knew that he had been given his choice.
hadith

When the prophet Muhammad heard someone say that he was superior to the prophet Jonah, he said, "Do not say that I am better than Jonah. Do not treat some of the prophets of God as superior to others."
hadith

When God intends to grant mercy to a people, among His servants He takes their prophet and makes him a forerunner who goes before them; but when He intends to destroy a people He punishes them while their prophet is alive, destroys them while he is there to see, and comforts him by their destruction when they disbelieved him and disobeyed his command.
hadith

Xian Mosque
Qingzhen, China

The Last Days

Among the signs of the last hour will be the removal of knowledge, the abundance of ignorance, the prevalence of fornication, the prevalence of wine-drinking, civil strife will appear, niggardliness will be cast into people's hearts, and slaughter will be prevalent.
hadith

The last hour will not come before the anti-Christ (al-dajjal) will come forth. While the best people on earth are preparing for battle and arranging their ranks the time for prayer will come and Jesus, son of Mary, will descend and lead them in prayer. When God's enemy sees him he (the anti-Christ) will dissolve like salt in water, and if he were to leave him he would dissolve completely; but God will kill him by his (Jesus, son of Mary's) hand and he will show them his blood on his spear.
hadith

Let me tell you something about the anti-Christ (al-dajjal) which no prophet has told his people. He is one-eyed, and will bring with him something like Paradise and hell, but what he calls Paradise will be hell. I warn you as Noah warned his people about him.
hadith

There is no prophet who has not warned his people about the one-eyed liar (the anti-Christ). I tell you that he is one-eyed, but your Lord is not one-eyed. On his forehead is the word "infidelity" (kufr), to which he summons people.
hadith

When the anti-Christ (al-dajjal) comes he will summon people and they will believe him. He will [produce miracles and turn people away from their religion. When his actions are the worst] God will send the Messiah, son of Mary, who will descend at the white minaret in the East of Damascus wearing two garments dyed with saffron and placing his hands on the wings of two angels. When he lowers his head it will drip and

[continued]

39

[continued]

when he raises it beads like pearls will scatter from it. Every infidel who feels the odor of his breath will die, and his breath will reach as far as he can see. He will then seek anti-Christ until he catches up with him and kills him. People whom God has protected from the anti-Christ will then come to Jesus who will wipe their faces and tell them of the ranks they will have in Paradise. While this is happening God will reveal to Jesus that He has brought forth servants of His with whom no one will be able to fight and tell him to collect His servants. God will then release Gog and Magog "and they will swarm down from every slope" [to create destruction]. God's prophet Jesus and his companions will then beseech God [to send various punishments to evildoers. After various punishments have occurred], God will send a pleasant wind which will take the righteous under their armpits and the spirit of every believer and every Muslim will be taken, but the wicked people will remain in the earth and will be disorderly like asses. Then the last hour will come to them.[3]
hadith

Last night I found myself in a vision at the Kaaba and I saw a ruddy man like the most good-looking of that type that you can see with the most beautiful lock of hair you can see. He had combed it out, and it was dripping with water. He was leaning on the shoulders of two men and going round the House (Kaaba). When I asked who he was I was told that he was the Messiah, son of Mary. Then I saw a man with short, woolly hair who was blind in the right eye, his eye looking like a floating grape. He was placing his hands on the shoulders of two men and going round the House. I asked who this man was and was told that he was the anti-Christ.
hadith

40

*Pulpit in the
Selemiye Djami
Mosque
Edirne, Turkey*

*Sultan Hassan Mosque
Cairo, Egypt*

Iman Mosque
Isfahan, Iran

Illuminated page from a Koran

The Day of Judgment, Paradise, and Hell

At the resurrection you will be assembled barefoot, naked, and uncircumcised. The first to be clothed on the Day of Resurrection will be Abraham. Then some of my companions will be taken to the left, and when I cry, "My little companions, my little companions!" I shall receive the reply that they have kept going back to infidelity since I left them.
hadith

Every prophet has a supplication which receives an answer, but whereas every prophet made his supplication in this world, I have kept mine until the Day of Judgment to be used in intercession for my people, and if God wills, it will reach those of my people who have died without associating anything with God.
hadith

Every prophet has a pond (in Paradise) and they will vie with one another about which of them will have the largest number coming down to it.
hadith

"The inhabitants of Paradise will look at those in the upper apartments above them as you look at a shining planet which remains in the East or West horizon, on account of the superiority some have over others." God's messenger was asked whether those were the dwellings of the prophets which no one else would reach, and replied, "Yes they will. By Him in whose hand my soul is, men who believed in God and acknowledged the truth of His messengers will reach them."
hadith

God will say to the inhabitant of hell who has the lightest punishment, "If you had everything the earth contains would you seek to ransom yourself with it?" and when he replies that he would, He will say, "I desired less than that from you when you were in Adam's loins—only that you should associate nothing with me." [4]
hadith

Ancient Messengers from God

Adam
Noah
Hud and the People of Ad
Salih and the People of Thamud
Shuaib and the People of Midian

Vault in the school of Tilia Kari
Samarkand, Uzbekistan

Adam

It is We who created you (mankind) and gave you shape. Then We bade the angels prostrate to Adam, and they prostrated; not so Iblis (Satan). He refused to be of those who prostrate. (God) said, "What prevented thee from prostrating when I commanded thee?" He said, "I am better than he (Adam); Thou didst create me from fire, and him from clay." (God) said, "Get thee down from this; it is not for thee to be arrogant here; get out, for thou art of the meanest (of creatures)."... He (Satan) said, "Because thou hast thrown me out of the way, verily I will lie in wait for them on Thy straight way. Then will I assault them from before them and behind them, from their right and their left; nor wilt thou find, in most of them, gratitude (for Thy mercies)."
7: 11-17

(God said) "O Adam! Dwell thou and thy wife in the Garden (of Eden) and eat from whence ye will, but come not nigh this tree lest ye become wrongdoers." Then Satan whispered to them that he might manifest unto them that which was hidden from them of their shame, and he said, "Your Lord forbade you from this tree only lest ye should become angels or become of the immortals." And he swore unto them (saying), "Verily I am a sincere adviser unto you." Thus did he lead them on with guile. And when they tasted of the tree their shame was manifest to them and they began to hide (by heaping) on themselves some of the leaves of the Garden. And their Lord called them, (saying), "Did I not forbid you from that tree and tell you, 'Verily Satan is an open enemy to you'?" They said, "Our Lord! We have wronged ourselves. If thou forgive us not and have not mercy on us, surely we are of the lost!" He said, "Go down (from hence), one of you a foe unto the other. There will be for you on earth a habitation and provision for a while. There shall ye live, and there shall ye die, and thence shall ye be brought forth. O Children of Adam! We have revealed unto you raiment to conceal your shame, and splendid vesture, but the raiment of righteousness, that is best." This is of the signs [ayat] of God, that they may remember. O Children of Adam! Let not Satan seduce you as he caused your (first) parents to go forth from the Garden and tore off from them their robe (of innocence) that he might manifest their shame to them. Verily he seeth you, he and his tribe, from whence ye see him not. Verily We made the evil ones friends (only) to those without faith.... O Children of Adam! Wear your beautiful apparel at every time and place of prayer, eat and drink, but waste not by excess, for God loveth not the wasters.... O Children of Adam when messengers of your own come unto you who narrate unto you My signs [ayat], then whosoever refraineth from evil and amendeth—there shall no fear come upon them neither shall they grieve.... Verily your Lord is God who created the heavens and the earth in six days, then mounted He the Throne. He covereth the night with the day, which is in haste to follow it, and hath made the sun and the moon and the stars subservient by His command. His verily is all creation and commandment. Blessed be God, the Lord of the worlds! (O mankind!) Call upon your Lord humbly and in secret. Verily He loveth not aggressors. Do no mischief on the earth, after it hath been set in order, but call on Him with fear and longing (in your hearts), for the mercy of God is (always) near to those who do good.

7: 19-56

Mausoleum of Mulay Ismail
Meknes, Morocco

Alcazar
Seville, Spain

God created Adam from a handful which he took from the whole of the earth; so the children of Adam are in accordance with the earth, some red, some white, some black, some a mixture, also smooth and rough, bad and good.

hadith

Noah

We sent Noah to his people (with a mission), "I have come to you with a clear warning: that ye serve none but God. Verily I do fear for you the penalty of a grievous day." But the chiefs of the unbelievers among his people said, "We see (in) thee nothing but a man like ourselves.... Nor do we see in you (and your followers) any merit above us, in fact we think ye are liars!" He (Noah) said, "O my people! See ye if I have a clear sign from my Lord, and that He hath sent mercy unto me from His own presence, but that the mercy hath been obscured from your sight? Shall we compel you to accept it when ye are averse to it?..." They said, "O Noah! Thou hast disputed with us, and (much) hast thou prolonged the dispute with us; now bring upon us what thou threatenest us with, if thou speakest the truth!"... It was revealed to Noah, "None of thy people will believe except those who have believed already! So grieve no longer over their (evil) deeds, but construct an Ark under Our eyes and Our inspiration, and address Me no (further) on behalf of those who are in sin, for they are about to be overwhelmed (in the flood)." Forthwith he (began) constructing the Ark. Every time that the chiefs of his people passed by him, they threw ridicule on him. He said, "If ye ridicule us now, we (in our turn) can look down on you with ridicule likewise!..." At length, behold! There came Our command, and the fountains of the earth gushed forth! We said, "Embark therein, of each kind two, male and female, and your family—except those against whom the word has already gone forth—and the believers." But only a few believed with him.... So the Ark floated with them on the waves (towering) like mountains.... Then the word went forth, "O earth! swallow up thy water, and O sky! withhold (thy rain)!" and the water abated, and the matter was ended. The Ark rested on Mount Judi, and the word went forth, "Away with those who do wrong!" Such are some

[continued]

[continued]

of the stories of the unseen, which We have revealed unto thee, before this—neither thou nor thy people knew them. So persevere patiently, for the end (Day of Judgment) is for those who are righteous.
11: 25-49

Hud and the People of Ad

To (the people of) Ad (We sent) Hud, one of their own brethren. He said, "O my people worship God—ye have no other god but Him. (Your other gods) ye do nothing but invent!..." They said, "O Hud! No clear (sign) hast thou brought us, and we are not the ones to desert our gods on thy word! Nor shall we believe in thee!..." He said, "I call God to witness, and do ye bear witness, that I am free from the sin of ascribing to Him other gods as partners!..." So when Our decree issued, We saved Hud and those who believed with him; by (special) grace from Ourselves We saved them from a severe penalty. Such were (the people of) Ad—they rejected the signs of their Lord and Cherisher, disobeyed His messengers, and followed the command of every powerful, obstinate transgressor.
11: 50-59

Salih and the People of Thamud

To (the people of) Thamud (We sent) Salih, one of their own brethren. He said, "O my people! Worship God, ye have no other god but Him. It is He who hath produced you from the earth and settled you therein, so ask forgiveness of Him, and turn to Him (in repentance), for my Lord is (always) near, ready to answer." They said, "O Salih! Thou hast been of us a center of our hopes hitherto! Dost thou (now) forbid us the worship of what our fathers worshipped? But we are really in suspicious doubt as to that to which thou invitest us." He said, "O my people! Do ye see? I have a clear (sign) from my Lord and He hath sent mercy unto me from Himself—who then can help me against God if I were to disobey Him? What then would ye add to my (portion) but perdition?..." When our decree issued, We saved Salih and those who believed with him—by (special)

[continued]

Saints in a pavilion
Persian miniature, c. 1553

أمر بكتابة

هذه الرقعة الشريفة مولانا

السلطان الأعظم والخاقان المعظم مالك رقاب

الأمم سلطان سلاطين العرب والعجم ملك ملوك العالم ظل

الله في أرضه وخليفته على عباده مظهر الحق اليقين بالبراهين

غياث الدنيا والدين سلطان سلاطين الاسلام والمسلمين

المؤيد من السماء المنصور على الأعداء خداسند محمد بن السلطان السعيد

أرغون خان بن السلطان السعيد أبا قاخان بن السلطان السعيد هولاكو

خان بن تولوي خان بن جنكز خان خلد الله دولته على ممر الدهور والمدا

بالبقاء الى يوم البعث والنشور على يدي وزيريه الأعظمين سلطاني

وزراء العالم مدبري الملك اعز الله انصارها وضاعف اقتدارهما

[continued]

grace from Ourselves—from the ignominy of that day. For thy Lord—He is the strong one, and able to enforce His will. The (mighty) blast overtook the wrongdoers, and they lay prostrate in their homes before the morning—as if they had never dwelt and flourished there. Ah! Behold! For the Thamud rejected their Lord and Cherisher! Ah! Behold! Removed (from sight) were the Thamud!

11: 61-68

Shuaib and the People of Midian

To the (people of) Midian (We sent) Shuaib, one of their own brethren. He said, "O my people! Worship God; ye have no other god but Him.... And, O my people! Give just measure and weight, nor withhold from the people the things that are their due, commit not evil in the land with intent to do mischief. That which is left you by God is best for you, if ye (but) believed!..." They said, "O Shuaib! Does thy (religion of) prayer command thee that we leave off the worship which our fathers practiced, or that we leave off doing what we like with our property? Truly, thou art the one that forbeareth with faults!" He said, "O my people! See ye whether I have a clear (sign) from my Lord, and He hath given me sustenance (pure and) good as from Himself?... And, O my people! Let not my dissent (from you) cause you to sin, lest ye suffer a fate similar to that of the people of Noah or of Hud or of Salih, nor are the people of Lot far off from you! But ask forgiveness of your Lord, and turn unto Him (in repentance), for my Lord is indeed full of mercy and loving-kindness." They said, "O Shuaib! Much of what thou sayest we do not understand! In fact among us we see that thou hast no strength! Were it not for thy family, we should certainly have stoned thee!..." When Our decree issued, We saved Shuaib and those who believed with him, by (special) mercy from Ourselves, but the (mighty) blast did seize the wrongdoers, and they lay prostrate in their homes by the morning—as if they had never dwelt and flourished there! Ah! Behold! How the Midian were removed (from sight) as were removed the Thamud!

11: 84-95

Illuminated page from a Koran
Iraq, c. 1306

The Abrahamic Tradition

Abraham
Lot
Joseph
Ishmael, Idris, Enoch, Elisha, Ezekiel, and Job

Abraham

Ye People of the Book (Jews, Christians, and Muslims)! Why dispute ye about Abraham, when the Torah and the Gospel were not revealed until after him? Have ye no understanding? Ah! Ye are those who fell to disputing (even) in matters of which ye had some knowledge! But why dispute ye in matters of which ye have no knowledge? It is God who knows, and ye who know not! Abraham was not a Jew nor yet a Christian; but he was true in faith, and bowed his will to God's; and he was not of the idolaters.
3: 65-67

Our messengers came to Abraham with glad tidings. They (greeted him) saying, "Peace!" He answered, "Peace!"... And his wife, who was standing (there), laughed when We gave her glad tidings of (the coming birth) of Isaac, and after him, of Jacob. She said, "Alas for me! Shall I bear a child, seeing I am an old woman, and my husband here is an old man? That would indeed be a wonderful thing!" They said, "Dost thou wonder at God's decree? The grace of God and His blessings on you, O ye people of the house, for He is indeed worthy of all praise, full of all glory!"
11: 69-73

Remember Abraham said ... "My Lord! Verily they (idols) have led many of mankind astray. But whoso followeth me, he verily is of me. And whoso disobeyeth me—still Thou art forgiving, merciful. Thou art indeed oft-forgiving, most merciful. Our Lord! Verily I have settled some of my posterity in an uncultivatable valley near unto Thy holy house (Kaaba), our Lord, that they may establish proper worship; so fill the hearts of some among men with love towards them, and feed them with fruits, so that they may give thanks. O our Lord! Truly Thou dost know what we conceal and what we reveal, for nothing whatever is hidden from God, whether on earth or in heaven. Praise be to God, who hath granted unto me in old age Ishmael and Isaac, for truly my Lord is He, the hearer of prayer! O my Lord! Make me one who establishes regular prayer, and also (raise such)

[(continued]

[continued]

among my offspring, O our Lord, and accept Thou my prayer. O our Lord!
Cover (us) with Thy forgiveness—me, my parents, and (all) believers—on
the Day that the Reckoning will be established!"
14: 35-41

Abraham was indeed a model, devoutly obedient to God, (and) true in
faith, and he joined not gods with God. He showed his gratitude for the
favors of God, who chose him, and guided him to a straight way. And
We gave him good in this world, and he will be, in the hereafter, in the
ranks of the righteous. So We have taught thee (Muhammad) the inspired
(message), "Follow the ways of Abraham, the true in faith; and he joined
not gods with God."
16: 120-123

There is for you an excellent example (to follow) in Abraham and those
with him, when they said to their people, "We are clear of you and of
whatever ye worship besides God. We have rejected you, and there has
arisen, between us and you, enmity and hatred forever, until ye believe in
God and Him alone."
60: 4

God's messenger used to commend his grandsons Hasan and Husain to
God's protection, saying, "With God's perfect words I commend you to
God's protection from every devil and poisonous creature and from every
evil eye." And he would say to his grandsons, "Your ancestor (Abraham)
used to commend Ishmael and Isaac to God's protection."
hadith

When God's messenger met Abraham on the night he was taken up to
heaven, Abraham said, "Convey my greeting to your people, Muhammad,
and tell them that Paradise has good soil and sweet water, that it consists
of level, treeless plains, and that its plants are 'Glory be to God'; 'Praise be
to God'; 'There is no god but God'; and 'God is most great.'"
hadith

Replica of the famous Nejjarine in Fez
Royal Palace, Rabat, Morocco

Tomb of the saint Subayda
Baghdad, Iraq

When a man came to the Prophet and addressed him as "best of all creatures," the Prophet responded saying, "That was Abraham."
hadith

 Lot

When Our messengers came to Lot, he was grieved on their account and felt himself powerless (to protect) them. He said, "This is a distressful day." And his people came rushing toward him, and they had been long in the habit of practicing abominations…. (The messengers) said, "O Lot! We are messengers from thy Lord! By no means shall they reach thee! Now travel with thy family while yet a part of the night remains, and let not any of you look back; but thy wife (will remain behind). To her will happen what happens to the people. Morning is their time appointed, is not the morning nigh?" So when Our decree came to pass, We turned (the cities) upside down, and rained down on them brimstones hard as baked clay, spread, layer on layer—marked with fire in the providence of thy Lord (for the destruction of the wicked).
11: 77-83

Tell them about the guests of Abraham…. Abraham said, "What then is the matter on which ye (have come), O ye messengers (of God)?"… They said, "We have been sent to a people (deep) in sin, excepting the followers of Lot—them we are certainly (charged) to save (from harm). [Then follows the story of Lot and the destruction of Sodom and Gomorrah.] Behold! In this is a sign for those who believed.
15: 51-77

God have mercy on Lot who sought refuge in a strong support.[5]
hadith

The thing I fear most for my people is what Lot's people did [in Sodom and Gomorrah].
hadith

Joseph

Behold! Joseph said to his father, "O my father! I did see eleven stars and the sun and the moon—I saw them prostrate themselves to me!" Said (the father), "My (dear) little son! Relate not thy vision to thy brothers, lest they concoct a plot against thee, for Satan is to man an avowed enemy! Thus will thy Lord choose thee and teach thee the interpretation of stories (and events) and perfect His favor to thee and to the posterity of Jacob, even as He perfected it to thy fathers Abraham and Isaac aforetime—for God is full of knowledge and wisdom." Verily in Joseph and his brethren are signs (or symbols) for seekers (after truth). [The story is related of Joseph's betrayal by his brothers when he was sold into slavery in Egypt.]... The man in Egypt who bought him, said to his wife, "Make his stay (among us) honorable; it may be he will bring us much good, or we shall adopt him as a son." Thus did We establish Joseph in the land, that We might teach him the interpretation of stories (and events). And God hath full power and control over His affairs; but most among mankind know it not. When Joseph attained his full manhood, We gave him power and knowledge; thus do We reward those who do right.... The king (of Egypt) said, "I do see (in a vision) seven fat cows, whom seven lean ones devour, and seven green ears of corn, and seven (others) withered. O ye chiefs, expound to me my vision if it be that ye can interpret visions." [The story is related of how Joseph was the only person to correctly predict the meaning of the king's dream.]... So the king said, "Bring him (Joseph) unto me; I will take him specially to serve about my own person." Therefore when he had spoken to him, he said, "Be assured this day, thou art, before our own presence, with rank firmly established, and fidelity fully proved!"

[It is then told how Joseph was given control over all the storehouses in Egypt.]... Then came Joseph's brethren, they entered his presence, and he knew them, but they knew him not. [Then the story is related of Joseph's reconciliation with his brothers and his father.]... Then when they (Joseph's family) entered the presence of Joseph, he provided a home for his parents with himself, and said, "Enter ye Egypt (all) in safety if it please God." And he raised his parents high on the throne (of dignity)....
He said, "O my father! This is the fulfillment of my vision of old! God hath

[continued]

Mausoleum of Khan Uljaitu Sultanate
Tabriz, Iraq, c. 1307-1313

made it come true! He was indeed good to me when He took me out of prison and brought you (all here) out of the desert, (even) after Satan had sown enmity between me and my brothers. Verily my Lord understandeth best the mysteries of all that He planneth to do, for verily He is full of knowledge and wisdom. O my Lord! Thou hast indeed bestowed on me some power, and taught me something of the interpretation of dreams and events. O Thou creator of the heavens and the earth! Thou art my protector in this world and in the hereafter. Take Thou my soul (at death) as one submitting to Thy will, and unite me with the righteous."
12: 4-101

When God's messenger was asked who among men was most honorable, he replied, "The one who is most honorable in God's estimation is the most pious." On being told that that was not what they meant, he said, "The most honorable was God's prophet Joseph, son of God's prophet Jacob, son of God's prophet Isaac, son of God's friend Abraham."
hadith

Ishmael, Idris, Enoch, Elisha, Ezekiel, and Job

Also mention in the Scripture (the story of) Ishmael: he was (strictly) true to what he promised, and he was a messenger (and) a prophet. He used to enjoin on his people prayer and charity, and he was most acceptable in the sight of his Lord.
19: 54-55

Also mention in the Scripture the case of Idris, Enoch: he was a man of truth (and sincerity), (and) a prophet, and We raised him to a lofty station.
19: 56-57

Iman Mosque
Isfahan, Iran

And (remember) Job, when he cried to his Lord, "Truly distress has seized me, but Thou art the most merciful of those that are merciful." Then We heard his prayer and removed that adversity from which he suffered, and We gave him his household (that he had lost) and the like thereof along with them, a mercy from Our store, and a remembrance for the worshippers.
21: 83-84

And (remember) Ishmael, and Enoch, and Ezekiel: all were of the steadfast and We brought them in unto Our mercy. Verily they are among the righteous.
21: 85-86

A small mausoleum
Turfan, China

Mausoleum of Aba Khoja
Kashgar, China

Commemorate Our servant Job.... Truly We found him full of patience and constancy. How excellent in Our service! Ever did he turn (to Us)! And commemorate Our servants Abraham, Isaac, and Jacob, possessors of power and vision. Verily We did choose them for a special (purpose) — proclaiming the message of the hereafter. They were, in Our sight, truly of the company of the elect and the good. And commemorate Ishmael, Elisha, and Ezekiel: each of them was of the company of the good.
38: 41-48

Judaism

Moses and Aaron
David
Solomon
The Children of Israel

Moses and Aaron

We sent Moses with Our signs to Pharaoh and his chiefs, but they wrongfully rejected them — so see what was the end of those who made mischief. Moses said, "O Pharaoh! I am a messenger from the Lord of the worlds — one for whom it is right to say nothing but truth about God. Now have I come unto you (people), from your Lord, with a clear (sign). So let the Children of Israel depart along with me." (Pharaoh) said, "If indeed thou hast come with a sign, show it forth — if thou tellest the truth." Then (Moses) threw down his rod, and behold! It was a serpent, plain (for all to see)!... Said the chiefs of the people of Pharaoh, "This is indeed a sorcerer well-versed...." So there came the sorcerers to Pharaoh.... When they (the Pharaoh's sorcerers) threw, they bewitched the eyes of the people, and struck terror into them, for they showed a great (feat of) magic. We put it into Moses' mind by inspiration, "Throw (now) thy rod," and behold! — it swallowed up straight away all the falsehoods which they faked! Thus truth was confirmed, and all that they did was made of no effect.... Said Pharaoh, "Believe ye in Him before I give you permission? Surely this is a trick...." Said the chiefs of Pharaoh's people, "Wilt thou leave Moses and his people, to spread mischief in the land, and to abandon thee and thy gods?" He said, "Their male children will we slay; (only) their females will we save alive; and we have over them (power) irresistible." Said Moses to his people, "Pray for help from God and (wait) in patience and constancy, for the earth is God's to give as a heritage to such of His servants as He pleaseth; and the end is (best) for the righteous." They said, "We have had (nothing but) trouble, both before and after thou camest to us." He (Moses) said, "It may be that your Lord will destroy your enemy and make you inheritors in the earth; that so He may try you by your deeds." We punished the people of Pharaoh with years (of droughts) and shortness of crops, that they might receive admonition.... The Pharaoh said (to Moses), "Whatever be the signs thou bringest, to work therewith thy sorcery on us, we shall never believe in thee." So We sent (plagues) on them, wholesale death, locusts, lice, frogs, and blood — signs openly self-explained. But they were steeped in arrogance — a people given to sin. Every time the penalty fell on them, they said, "O Moses! On your behalf call on thy Lord in virtue of His promise to thee. If thou wilt remove the penalty from

[continued]

[continued]

us, we shall truly believe in thee, and we shall send away the Children of Israel with thee." But every time We removed the penalty from them according to a fixed term which they had to fulfill—behold! They broke their word! So We exacted retribution from them. We drowned them in the sea, because they rejected Our signs and failed to take warning from them. And We made a people, considered weak (and of no account), inheritors of lands in both East and West—lands whereon We sent down Our blessings. The fair promise of thy Lord was fulfilled for the Children of Israel, because they had patience and constancy, and We leveled to the ground the great works and fine buildings which Pharaoh and his people erected (with such pride). We took the Children of Israel (with safety) across the sea. They came upon a people devoted entirely to some idols they had.

Mausoleum of Imam Hussein
Kerbela, Iraq

They said, "O Moses! Fashion for us a god like unto the gods they have."
He said, "Surely ye are a people without knowledge...." We appointed for
Moses thirty nights, and completed (the period) with ten (more); thus
was completed the term (of communion) with his Lord—forty nights.
And Moses had charged his brother Aaron (before he went up), "Act for
me among my people—do right, and follow not the way of those who
do mischief." When Moses came to the place appointed by Us, and his
Lord addressed him, he said, "O my Lord! Show (Thyself) to me, that I
may look upon thee." God said, "By no means canst thou see Me (direct).
But look upon the mount—if it abide in its place, then shalt thou see

[continued]

[continued]

Me." When his Lord manifested His glory on the mount, He made it as dust. And Moses fell down senseless. When he recovered his senses he said, "Glory be to Thee! To Thee I turn in repentance, and I am the first to believe." God said, "O Moses! I have chosen thee above (other) men, by the messages I (have given thee) and the words I (have spoken to thee); take then that which I have given thee, and be of those who give thanks." And We ordained laws for him in the tablets in all matters, both commanding and explaining all things, (and said), "Take and hold these with firmness, and enjoin thy people to hold fast by the best in the precepts...." The people of Moses made, in his absence, out of their ornaments, the image of a calf (for worship)... (that) seemed to moo. Did they not see that it could neither speak to them, nor show them the way? They took it for worship and they did wrong.... Those who took the calf (for worship) will indeed be overwhelmed with wrath from their Lord, and with shame in this life—thus do We recompense those who invent (falsehoods).... When the anger of Moses was appeased, he took up the tablets; in the writing thereon was guidance

and mercy for such as fear their Lord.... Of the people of Moses there is a section who guide and do justice in the light of truth. We divided them into twelve tribes or nations. We directed Moses by inspiration, when his (thirsty) people asked him for water, (saying), "Strike the rock with thy staff" — out of it there gushed forth twelve springs. Each group knew its own place for water. We gave them the shade of clouds, and sent down to them manna and quails, (saying), "Eat of the good things We have provided for you." (But they rebelled); to Us they did no harm, but they harmed their own souls.... But the transgressors among them changed the word from that which had been given them so we sent on them a plague from heaven. For that they repeatedly transgressed.... We broke them up into sections on this earth. There are among them some that are the righteous, and some that are the opposite. We have tried them with both prosperity and adversity, in order that they might turn (to us). After them succeeded an (evil) generation. They inherited the Book (Torah), but they chose (for themselves) the vanities of this world, saying (for excuse), "(Everything) will be forgiven us."... As to those who hold fast by the Book and establish regular prayer — never shall We suffer the reward of the righteous to perish.
7: 103-170

Chellah Mosque
Rabat, Morocco

It was We who revealed the Torah—therein was guidance and light. By its standard have been judged the Jews, by the prophets who submitted to God's will, by the rabbis and the doctors of law—for to them was entrusted the protection of God's Book (Torah) and they were witnesses thereto. Therefore fear not men, but fear Me, and sell not My signs for a miserable price. If any do fail to judge by (the light of) what God hath revealed, they are unbelievers.[6]

5: 44

We narrate unto thee some of the story of Moses and Pharaoh with truth, for folk who believe. Verily Pharaoh exalted himself in the earth and broke up its people into sections. A tribe among them he oppressed, killing their sons and sparing their women. Verily he was of those who work corruption. And We desired to show favor unto those who were oppressed in the earth, and to make them examples and to make them the inheritors. So We inspired the mother of Moses, saying, "Suckle him and, when thou fearest for him, then cast him into the river and fear not nor grieve. Verily We shall bring him back unto thee and shall make him (one) of Our messengers." And the family of Pharaoh took him up, that he might become for them an enemy and a sorrow.... And the wife of Pharaoh said, "(He will be) a

Mosque of Sidi Bu Makhluf
Al-Kaf, Tunisia

consolation for me and for thee. Kill him not. Peradventure he may be of use to us, or we may choose him for a son." And they perceived not. But there came to be a void in the heart of the mother of Moses—she was going almost to disclose his (case), had We not strengthened her heart (with faith) so that she might remain a (firm) believer. And she said to the sister of (Moses), "Follow him"; so she (the sister) watched him in the character of a stranger. And they knew not. So We restored him to his mother that she might be comforted and not grieve, and that she might know that the promise of God is true; but most of them know not. When he reached full age and was firmly established (in life), We bestowed on him wisdom and knowledge, for thus do We reward those who do good. [The story is related of Moses slaying a wicked Egyptian who was fighting with a Jew, with the result that Moses had to flee for his life.]... He therefore got away therefrom, looking about, in a state of fear. He prayed: "O my Lord! Save me from people given to wrongdoing." Then ... he turned his face towards (the land of) Midian.... And when he arrived at the watering (place) in Midian, he found there a group of men watering (their flocks), and besides them he found two women who were keeping back (their flocks). He said, "What is the matter with you?" They

[continued]

Grand Mosque
Chaouen, Morocco

Grand Mosque
Ouezzane, Morocco

Koran illumination
India

[continued]

said, "We cannot water (our flocks) until the shepherds take back (their flocks), and our father is a very old man." So he watered (their flocks) for them; then he turned back to the shade and said, "O my Lord! Truly am I in (desperate) need of any good that Thou dost send me!" Afterwards one of the (damsels) came (back) to him, walking bashfully. She said, "My father invites thee that he may reward thee for having watered (our flocks) for us." So when he came to him and narrated the story, he said, "Fear thou not, (well) hast thou escaped from unjust people."... He said, "I intend to wed one of these my daughters to thee, on condition that thou serve me for eight years; but if thou complete ten years, it will be (grace) from thee. But I intend not to place thee under a difficulty; thou wilt find me, indeed, if God wills, one of the righteous."... Now when Moses had fulfilled the term and was traveling with his family, he perceived a fire in the direction of Mount Sinai. He said to his family, "Tarry ye; I perceive a fire; I hope to bring you from there some information, or a burning firebrand, that ye may warm yourselves." But when he came to the (fire), a voice was heard from the right bank of the valley, from a tree in hallowed ground, "O Moses! Verily I am God, the Lord of the worlds.... Now do thou throw thy rod!" But when he saw it moving (of its own accord) as if it had been a snake, he turned back in retreat, and retraced not his steps. "O Moses! Draw near, and fear not, for thou art of those who are secure.... Those are the two credentials from thy Lord to Pharaoh and his chiefs, for truly they are a people rebellious and wicked." He said, "O my Lord! I have slain a man among them, and I fear lest they slay me. And my brother Aaron—he is more eloquent in speech than I, so send him with me as a helper, to confirm (and strengthen) me, for I fear that they may accuse me of falsehood." God said, "We will certainly strengthen thy arm through thy brother, and invest you both with authority, so they shall not be able to touch you; with Our sign shall ye triumph—you two as well as those who follow you." When Moses came to them with Our clear signs, they said, "This is nothing but fabricated sorcery, never did we hear the like among our fathers of old!" [The story is told of Pharaoh's refusal to accept the signs.]... So We seized him and his hosts, and We flung them into the sea. Now behold what was the end of those who did wrong!
28: 3-40

Prayer hall of the
Grand Mosque of Gulbarga
Deccan, India c. 1365-1370

Moses was a modest man who kept himself covered, none of his skin being seen because of modesty. Some of the Jews annoyed him by saying that he concealed himself to this extent only because of some skin trouble such as leprosy, but God wished to clear him. So one day when he was alone having a bath he placed his garment on a stone and the stone flew away with his garment. Moses raced after it saying, "My garment, stone; my garment, stone," until he came to a company of some Jews who, seeing him naked in the most beautiful form God had created, said, "We swear by God that there is nothing wrong with Moses." He took his garment and began to beat the stone, and I swear by God that there were three, four, or five scars on the stone from the effect of his beating.
hadith

The angel of death came to Moses, son of Imran, and told him to answer his Lord's summons; whereupon Moses gave the angel of death a blow in the eye and knocked it out. The angel then returned to God Most High and said, "Thou didst send me to a servant of Thine who does not wish to die, and he has put out my eye." God restored his eye to him and said, "Go back to My servant and ask him if it is life he wants; then tell him that if he wants life he must place his hand on an ox's back, and he will live a year for every hair which covers his hand." Moses asked what would happen after that, and when he was told that he would die, he said, "Let it be now without delay. My Lord, bring me within a stone's throw of the Holy Land." God's messenger said, "I swear by God that if I were there I would show you his grave beside the road at the red mound."
hadith

God's messenger (Muhammad) came to Medina and found the Jews observing the fast on the day of Ashura, so he asked them what was the significance of that day. They replied, "It is a great day on which God delivered Moses and his people and drowned Pharaoh and his people; so Moses observed it as a fast out of gratitude, and we do so also." The Prophet said, "We have as close a connection with Moses as you have," so God's messenger observed it as a fast himself and gave orders that it should be observed.
hadith

Moses asked his Lord to teach him something with which to make mention of Him or to supplicate Him, and was told to say, "There is no god but God." Moses replied to his Lord that all His servants said this, but he wanted something particularly for himself, and He said, "Moses, were the seven heavens and the seven earths and their inhabitants put in one side of a balance and 'There is no god but God' in the other, 'There is no god but God' would outweigh them."
hadith

A man among the Muslims and a man among the Jews hated one another. The Muslim said, "By Him who chose Muhammad above the universe," and the Jew said, "By Him who chose Moses above the universe." Thereupon the Muslim raised his hand and struck the Jew on his face, and the Jew went to the Prophet and told him what had happened. The Prophet summoned the Muslim and confirmed the circumstance. The Prophet then said, "Do not make me superior to Moses, for mankind will fall down senseless on the Day of Resurrection and I shall fall down senseless along with them. I shall be the first to recover and shall see Moses seizing the side of the Throne; and I shall not know whether he was among those who fell senseless and had recovered before me, or whether he was among those of whom God had exempted from [this]."[7]
hadith

Moses asked, "My Lord, who is the greatest of Thy servants in Thy estimation?" and received the reply, "The one who forgives when he is in a position of power."
hadith

Being given information is not like seeing. God Most High gave Moses information about what his people had done regarding the (golden) calf and he did not throw down the tablets; but when he saw what they did, he threw down the tablets and they were broken.
hadith

David

When they advanced to meet Goliath and his forces, they prayed: "Our Lord! Pour out constancy on us and make our steps firm; help us against those that reject faith." By God's will they routed them; and David slew Goliath; and God gave him power and wisdom and taught him whatever (else) He willed. And did not God check one set of people by means of another, the earth would indeed be full of mischief—but God is full of bounty to all the worlds.

2: 250-251

Fountain in the Royal Palace
Meknes, Morocco

We did bestow on some prophets more (and other) gifts than on others, and We gave to David the Psalms.
17: 55

And assuredly We gave David grace from Us, (saying), "O ye mountains and birds, echo his Psalms of praise!"
34: 10

Remember our servant David, the man of strength, for he ever turned (to God). It was We that made the hills declare, in unison with him, Our praises, at eventide and at break of day; and the birds gathered (in assemblies), all with him did turn (to God). We strengthened his kingdom, and gave him wisdom and sound judgment in speech and decision. [The story of two disputing brothers is told.]... O David! We did indeed make thee a vice-regent on earth, so judge thou between men in truth (and justice).
38: 17-26

Recitation of Scripture was made easy for David, who would order his beasts to be saddled and would recite the Scripture before they had been saddled; and he would eat only what his hands had earned.
hadith

Mosque of Ibn Tulun
Cairo, Egypt

The prayer dearest to God is David's and the fasting dearest to God is David's. He would sleep half the night, get up to pray for a third of it, then sleep the remaining sixth; and he would fast on alternate days.
hadith

David had an hour during the night in which he would waken his family and say, "Family of David, get up and pray, for this is an hour in which God who is great and glorious answers petitions, except to a magician or a tax-gatherer."
hadith

Part of David's supplication was that he would say, "O God, I ask Thee for Thy love, the love of those who love Thee, and deeds which will cause me to attain to Thy love. O God, make Thy love dearer to me than myself, my property, my family, and than cold water."
hadith

When God's messenger mentioned David and talked about him, he would say that, "David was, of men, the most devoted to worship."
hadith

No one has ever eaten better food than what he eats as a result of the labor of his hands. God's prophet David used to eat from what he had worked for with his hands.
hadith

Mosque of Al-Maridani
Cairo, Egypt

The Dome of the Rock
Jerusalem

Solomon

(It was Our power that made) the violent (unruly) wind flow (tamely) for Solomon, to his order, to the land which We had blessed, for We do know all things.
21: 81

We indeed gave knowledge to David and Solomon, and they both said, "Praise be to God, who has favored us above many of His servants who believe!" And Solomon was David's heir. He said, "O ye people! We have been taught the speech of birds, and on us has been bestowed (abundance) of all things; this is indeed grace manifest (from God)." [The story of Solomon and the queen of Sheba is told.]... And he (Solomon) diverted her (the queen of Sheba) from the worship of others besides God, for she was of a people that had no faith. She said, "My Lord! Verily I have wronged myself, and I surrender with Solomon unto God, the Lord of the worlds."
27: 15-44

And to Solomon (We made) the wind (obedient), whereof the morning course was a month's journey and the evening course a month's journey.
34: 12

To David We gave Solomon (for a son)—how excellent in Our service! Ever did he turn (to Us)!... And We did try Solomon.... And he enjoyed, indeed, a near approach to Us, and a beautiful place of (final) return.
38: 30-40

The Children of Israel

O Children of Israel! Call to mind the (special) favor which I bestowed upon you, and fulfill your covenant with Me as I fulfill My covenant with

you, and fear none but Me; and believe in what I reveal, confirming the revelation which is with you; and be not the first to reject faith therein, nor sell My signs for a small price; and fear Me, and Me alone.
2: 40-41

Because of the wrongdoing of the Jews We forbade them good things which were (before) made lawful unto them, and because of their much hindering from God's way, and of their taking usury when they were forbidden it, and of their devouring people's wealth by false pretenses. We have prepared for those of them who disbelieve a painful doom. But those of them who are firm in knowledge and the believers (who) believe in that which is revealed unto thee (O Muhammad) and that which was revealed before thee—especially the diligent in prayer and those who pay the poor-due, the believers in God and the Last Day—upon these We shall bestow immense reward.
4: 160-162

Verily this is a revelation from the Lord of the worlds. With it came down the faithful Spirit upon thy heart, that thou mayest admonish in a clear, Arabic tongue. Truly it is in the Scriptures of the ancients.... Is it not a sign to them that the learned of the Children of Israel knew it (as true)? Had We revealed it to those (who did not speak Arabic), and had he (Muhammad) recited it to them, they would not have believed in it.
26: 192-199

And verily we gave the Children of Israel the Scripture (Torah) and the Judgment, and prophethood, and provided them with good things and favored them above (all) peoples; and gave them plain commandments. And they differed not until after the knowledge came unto them, through rivalry among themselves. Verily thy Lord will judge between them on the Day of Resurrection concerning that wherein they used to differ.
45: 16-17

Christianity

The Story of Jesus' Life
Jesus
The Virgin Mary
John the Baptist
Christians

CHRISTIANITY

Behold! The angels said, "O Mary! God hath chosen thee and purified thee—chosen thee above the women of all nations. O Mary! Worship thy Lord devoutly, prostrate thyself, and bow down (in prayer) with those who bow down."... Behold! The angels said, "O Mary! God giveth thee glad tidings of a Word from Him: his name will be Messiah Jesus, the son of Mary, held in honor in this world and the hereafter and of (the company of) those nearest to God. He shall speak to the people in childhood and in maturity. And he shall be (of the company) of the righteous." She said, "O my Lord! How shall I have a son when no man hath touched me?" He said, "Even so. God createth what He willeth. When He hath decreed a plan, He but saith to it, 'Be,' and it is!" And He will teach him (Jesus) the Scripture and wisdom, and the Torah and the Gospel, and (appoint him) a messenger to the Children of Israel, (with this message), "I have come to you, with a sign from your Lord, in that I make for you out of clay, as it were, the figure of a bird, and breathe into it, and it becomes a bird by God's leave. And I heal those born blind, and the lepers, and I quicken the dead, by God's leave; and I declare to you what ye eat, and what ye store in your houses. Surely therein is a sign for you if ye did believe. (I have come to you), to attest the law which was before me and to make lawful to you part of what was (before) forbidden to you; I have come to you with a sign from your Lord. So fear God, and obey me."... When Jesus found unbelief on their part, he said, "Who will be my helpers to (the work of) God?" Said the disciples, "We are God's helpers. We believe in God, and do thou bear witness that we have surrendered (unto Him)...." (And remember) when God said, "O Jesus! Verily I am gathering thee and causing thee to ascend unto Me, and am cleansing thee of those who disbelieve and am setting those who follow thee above those who disbelieve until the Day of Resurrection. Then unto Me ye will (all) return, and I shall judge between you as to that wherein ye used to differ."
3: 42-55

They (who) rejected faith—they uttered against Mary a grave false charge. And they said (in boast), "We killed Messiah Jesus, the son of Mary, the messenger of God." But they killed him not, nor crucified him, but so it was made to appear to them; and those who differ therein are full of doubts, with no (certain) knowledge, but only conjecture to follow, for of a surety they killed him not. Nay, God raised him up unto Himself—God is exalted in power, wise—and there is none of the People of the Book but must believe in him (Jesus) before his (own) death; and on the Day of Judgment he will be a witness against them.
4: 156-159

Relate in the Book (the story of) Mary, when she withdrew from her family to a place in the east. She placed a screen (to screen herself) from them; then We sent her our angel, and he appeared before her as a man in all respects.... He said, "Nay, I am only a messenger from thy Lord, (to announce) to thee the gift of a holy son." She said, "How shall I have a son, seeing that no man has touched me, and I am not unchaste?" He said, "So (it will be). Thy Lord saith, 'That is easy for Me, and (We wish) to appoint him as a sign unto men and a mercy from Us.' It is a matter (so) decreed." So she conceived him, and she retired with him to a remote place. [The birth of Jesus is related and the return of Mary to her people.]... She pointed to the babe. They said, "How can we talk to one who is a child in the cradle?" He (Jesus) said, "And He hath made me blessed wheresoever I be, and hath enjoined on me prayer and charity as long as I live. I am indeed a servant of God, He hath given me the Scripture and made me a prophet...." Such (was) Jesus, the son of Mary. (It is) a statement of truth, about which they (vainly) dispute. It befitteth not (the majesty of) God that He should take unto Himself a son. Glory be to Him! When He determines a matter, He only says to it, "Be," and it is.
19: 16-35

God's messenger (Muhammad) spoke of a prophet who, when his people beat him and covered him with blood, was wiping the blood from his face and saying, "O God, forgive my people, for they do not know."
hadith

Prayer hall entrance
Aljaferia Palace
Saragossa, Spain

Selemiye Djami Mosque
Edirne, Turkey

CHRISTIANITY

Those messengers We endowed with gifts, some above others; to some of them God spoke; others He raised to degrees (of honor); to Jesus, the son of Mary, We gave clear (signs), and strengthened him with the Holy Spirit.
2: 253

Verily the likeness of Jesus with God is as the likeness of Adam. He created him of dust, then He said unto him: "Be!" and he was.
3: 59

Do not exaggerate in your religion nor utter anything concerning God save the truth. The Messiah, Jesus, son of Mary, was only a messenger of God, and His Word which He conveyed unto Mary, and a Spirit from Him. So believe in God and His messengers, and say not "Three"—cease! (It is) better for you!—God is only One God.[8]
4: 171

And We caused Jesus, son of Mary, to follow in their footsteps, confirming that which was (revealed) before him in the Torah; and We bestowed on him the Gospel wherein is guidance and a light, confirming that which was (revealed) before it in the Torah—a guidance and an admonition unto those who fear God. Let the People of the Gospel judge by that which God hath revealed therein. Whoso judgeth not by that which God hath revealed—such are evil livers. And unto thee (O Muhammad) have We revealed the Scripture with the truth, confirming whatever Scripture was before it, and a watcher over it.
5: 46-48

They surely disbelieve who say, "Verily God is the Messiah, son of Mary." The Messiah (Jesus) said, "O Children of Israel, worship God, my Lord and your Lord. Verily whoso ascribeth partners unto God, for him God hath forbidden Paradise." They surely disbelieve who say, "Verily God is one of three in a Trinity," when there is no God save the One God. If they desist not from so saying, a painful doom will fall on those of them who

[continued]

[continued]
disbelieve.... The Messiah, son of Mary, was no other than a messenger, messengers (the like of whom) had passed away before him, and his mother was a saintly woman—and they both used to eat (earthly) food. See how We make the revelations clear for them, and see how they are turned away!
5: 72-75

One day will God gather the messengers together, and ask, "What was the response ye received (from men to your teaching)?" They will say, "We have no knowledge—it is Thou who knowest in full all that is hidden." Then will God say, "O Jesus, son of Mary! Recount My favor to thee and to thy mother. Behold! I strengthened thee with the Holy Spirit, so that thou didst speak to the people in childhood and in maturity. Behold! I taught thee the Scripture and wisdom, the Torah and the Gospel. And behold! Thou makest out of clay, as it were, the figure of a bird, by My leave, and thou breathest into it and it becometh a bird by My leave, and thou healest those born blind, and the lepers, by My leave. And behold! Thou bringest forth the dead by My leave."... And behold! God will say, "O Jesus, son of Mary! Didst thou say unto men, 'Worship me and my mother as gods in derogation of God'?" He (Jesus) will say, "Glory to Thee! Never could I say what I had no right (to say). Had I said such a thing, Thou wouldst indeed have known it. Thou knowest what is in my heart, though I know not what is in Thine. For Thou knowest in full all that is hidden."
5: 109-116

O ye who believe! Be ye helpers of God, as said Jesus, the son of Mary, to the disciples, "Who will be my helpers to (the work of) God?" Said the disciples, "We are God's helpers!" Then a portion of the Children of Israel believed, and a portion disbelieved; but We gave power to those who believed, against their enemies, and they became the ones that prevailed.
61: 14

If anyone testifies that there is no god but God alone, who has no partner, that Muhammad is His servant and messenger, that Jesus is God's servant and messenger, the son of His handmaid, His Word which he cast into Mary and a Spirit from Him, and that Paradise and hell are real, then God will cause him to enter Paradise no matter what he has done.
hadith

All the descendants of Adam have their sides pierced by the devil with two of his fingers at birth, except the son of Mary.
hadith

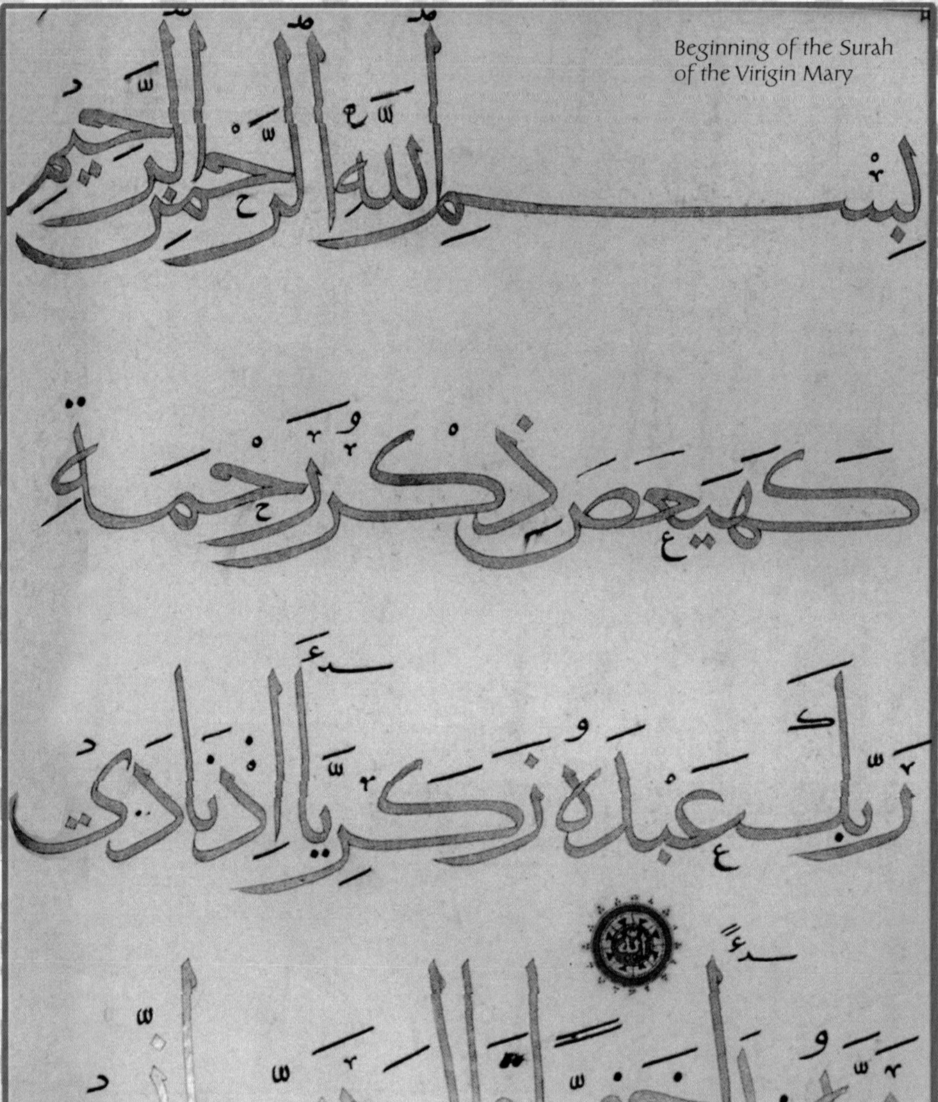

بسم الله الرحمن الرحيم
كهيعص ذكر رحمة
ربك عبده زكريا اذ نادى
ربه ندا خفيا قال رب انى

Beginning of the Surah
of the Virigin Mary

The Virgin Mary

Behold! A woman of (the family of) Imran said, "O my Lord! I do dedicate unto Thee what is in my womb for Thy special service, so accept this of me — for Thou hearest and knowest all things." When she was delivered, she said: "O my Lord! Behold! I am delivered of a female child!... I have named her Mary, and I commend her and her offspring to Thy protection from the Evil One, the rejected." Right graciously did her Lord accept her. He made her grow in purity and beauty. To the care of Zachariah (father of John the Baptist) was she assigned. Whenever Zachariah went in to her in the sanctuary, he found her provisioned. He said: "O Mary! Whence (comes) this to you?" She said, "From God, for God provides sustenance to whom He pleases without measure."
3: 35-37

And (remember) she who guarded her chastity, We breathed into her of Our Spirit, and We made her and her son a sign for all peoples.
21: 91

And (remember) Mary, daughter of Imran, who guarded her virginity, so We breathed into her of Our Spirit, and she confirmed the Words of her Lord and His Books, and was one of the devout.
66: 12

Many men have been perfect, but among women only Mary, the daughter of Imran, and Asiya, the wife of a Pharaoh (of Egypt), were perfect.
hadith

Except Mary and her son (Jesus), no human being is born without the devil touching him, so that he raises his voice crying out because of the devil's touch.
hadith

(This is) a recital of the mercy of thy Lord to His servant Zachariah. Behold! He cried to his Lord in secret, praying, "O my Lord! Infirm indeed are my bones, and the hair of my head doth glisten with gray; but never am I unblest, O my Lord, in my calling upon Thee! I fear my kinsfolk after me, since my wife is barren. Oh, give me from Thy presence a successor. (One that) will (truly) represent me, and represent the posterity of Jacob; and make him, O my Lord! one with whom Thou art well pleased!" (His prayer was answered), "O Zachariah! We give thee good news of a son—his name shall be John; on none by that name have We conferred distinction before." He said, "O my Lord! How shall I have a son, when my wife is barren and I have grown quite decrepit from old age?" God said, "So (it will be)."... (Zachariah) said, "O my Lord! Give me a sign." "Thy sign shall be that thou shalt speak to no man for three nights, although thou art not dumb." [The story of John the Baptist's birth and righteousness is related.] ... So peace on him the day he was born, the day that he dies, and the day that he will be raised up to life (again)!
19: 2-15

And remember Zachariah, when he cried unto his Lord, "My Lord! Leave me not childless, though Thou art the best of inheritors." Then We heard his prayer, and bestowed upon him John. We cured his wife's (barrenness) for him. These (three) were ever quick in emulation in good works; they used to call on Us and called upon Us out of yearning and awe, and they were humble to Us.
21: 89-90

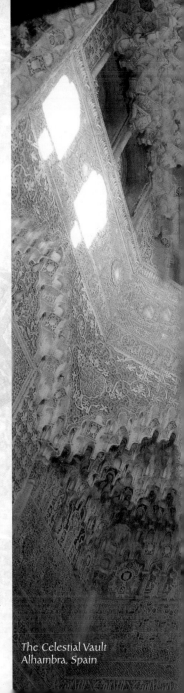

The Celestial Vault
Alhambra, Spain

Christians

And with those who say: "Lo! we are Christians," We made a covenant, but they have forgotten a portion of that which they were reminded of —so we estranged them, with enmity and hatred between the one and the other, till the Day of Resurrection; and God will assuredly tell them of the things they have done.

5: 14

Prayer niche of the Sale Madrassah, Morocco

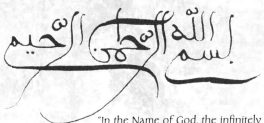

بسم الله الرحمن الرحيم

"In the Name of God, the infinitely Good, the ever Merciful"

Thou wilt surely find that the nearest ... in love to the believers (Muslims) are those who say, "We are Christians"; that is because there are priests and monks among them, and because they are not proud.
5: 82

Santa Maria
The White
Toledo, Spain

"People of the Book"

Those who believe (in the Koran), and those who follow the Jewish (Torah), and the Christians and the Sabians—any who believe in God and the Last Day, and work righteousness, shall have their reward with their Lord; on them shall be no fear, nor shall they grieve.
2: 62

And they say, "None entereth Paradise unless he be a Jew or a Christian." These are their own desires. Say, "Bring your proof (of what ye state) if ye are truthful." Nay, but whosoever surrendereth his purpose to God while doing good, his reward is with his Lord; and there shall no fear come upon them neither shall they grieve. And the Jews say the Christians follow nothing (true), and the Christians say the Jews follow nothing (true); yet both are readers of the Scripture. Even thus speak those who know not. God will judge between them on the Day of Resurrection concerning that wherein they differ.
2: 111-113

Of the People of the Book are a portion that stand (for the right). They rehearse the signs of God all night long, and they prostrate themselves in adoration. They believe in God and the Last Day; they enjoin what is right and forbid what is wrong; and they hasten (in emulation) in (all) good works. They are in the ranks of the righteous. Of the good that they do, nothing will be rejected of them—for God knoweth well those that do right.
3: 113-115

And there are, certainly, among the People of the Book, those who believe in God, in the revelation to you, and in the revelation to them, bowing in humility to God—they will not sell the signs of God for a miserable gain! For them is a reward with their Lord, and God is swift in account.
3: 199

The People of the Book ask thee to cause a book to descend to them from heaven; indeed they asked Moses for an even greater (miracle), for they said, "Show us God in public. But they were dazed for their presumption, with thunder and lightning. Yet they worshipped the calf even after clear signs had come to them; even so we forgave them, and gave Moses manifest proofs of authority. And for their covenant we raised over them (the towering height) of Mount (Sinai); and (on another occasion) we said, "Enter the gate with humility"; and (once again) we commanded them, "Transgress not in the matter of the Sabbath." And we took from them a solemn covenant. (They have incurred divine displeasure) in that they broke their covenant; that they rejected the signs of God; that they slew the messengers in defiance of right; that they said, "Our hearts are the wrappings (which preserve God's Word; we need no more)." Nay, God hath set the seal on their hearts for their blasphemy, so that they believe not save a few.
4: 153-155

If only the People of the Book would believe and ward off (evil), surely We should remit their sins from them and surely We should bring them into gardens of delight. If they had observed the Torah and the Gospel and that which was revealed unto them from their Lord, they would surely have been nourished from above them and from beneath their feet. Among them there are people who are moderate, but many of them are of evil conduct.... Say: O People of the Book! Ye have naught (of guidance) until ye observe the Torah and the Gospel and that which was revealed unto you from your Lord." That which is revealed unto thee (Muhammad) from thy Lord is certain to increase the contumacy and disbelief of many of them. But grieve not for the disbelieving folk. Verily those who believe, and those who are Jews, and Sabians, and Christians—whosoever believeth in God and the Last Day and doeth right—there shall no fear come upon them, neither shall they grieve.
5: 65-69

Arrival of the Prince
Persian miniature

Medallion containing an inscription of the name of the Prophet Muhammad

When the funeral bier of a Jew, a Christian, or a Muslim passes you, stand up for it. You are not standing for its sake, but for the angels who are accompanying it.
hadith

You will come to folk who are people of a Book (Jews and Christians), so invite them to testify that there is no god but God and that Muhammad is God's messenger. If they obey that, tell them God has made obligatory for them five times of prayer every twenty-four hours. If they obey that, tell them God has made obligatory for them charity to be taken from their rich and handed over to their poor. If they obey that, avoid taking the best parts of their property; and regard the claim of him who is wronged, for there is no veil between them and God.
hadith

When the Prophet went to his bed he used to say, "O God, Lord of the heavens, Lord of the earth, Lord of everything, who splittest the grain and the kernel, who hast sent down the Torah, the inspired statements of Jesus (Gospel), and the Koran, I seek refuge in Thee from the evil of every evil agent whose forelock Thou seizest. Thou art the First and there is nothing before Thee; Thou art the Last and there is nothing after Thee; Thou art the Outward and there is nothing above Thee; Thou art the Inward and there is nothing below Thee."
hadith

When the People of the Book salute you say, "The same to you.⁹
hadith

Does any of you imagine that God has prohibited only what is to be found in the Koran? By God, I have commanded, exhorted, and prohibited various matters as numerous as what is found in the Koran, or more numerous. God has not permitted you to enter the houses of the People of the Book (Jews and Christians) without permission; nor dishonor their women, nor eat their fruits, when they give you what is imposed on them.
hadith

Universal Truths from the Koran

Seek help in patience and prayer; and truly it is hard — save for the humble, who know that they will have to meet their Lord and that unto Him they are returning.
2: 45-46

Unto God belong the east and the west, and whithersoever ye turn, there is God's countenance. Verily God is All-embracing, All-knowing.
2: 115

Remember Me; I will remember you.
2: 152

We shall certainly test you with something of fear and hunger, and decrease of goods and lives and fruits, but assure those who are patient in adversity, who when calamity befalls them assert, "Surely we belong to God and surely we are returning to Him." Upon these shall flow their Lord's blessings and mercy, and they are the rightly guided.
2: 155-157

Your God is One God; there is no God save Him, the Beneficent, the Merciful.
2: 163

Behold! In the creation of the heavens and the earth; in the alternation of the night and the day; in the sailing of the ships through the ocean for the profit of mankind; in the rain which God sends down from the skies, and the life which He gives therewith to an earth that is dead;.in the beasts of all kinds that He scatters through the earth; in the change of the winds, and in the clouds which are pressed into service between the sky and the earth — (here) indeed are signs for a people that are wise.
2: 164

God! There is no god but He, the Living, the Self-subsisting. Neither slumber nor sleep overtaketh Him. Unto Him belongeth whatsoever is in the heavens and whatsoever is in the earth. Who is he that intercedeth with Him save by His leave? He knows what lies before them and what is after them, and they comprehend not anything of His knowledge save such as He wills. His throne extends over the heavens and the earth, and He is never burdened by preserving them. He is the Most-High, the All-glorious.
2: 255

Verily religion with God (is) surrender (to His will and guidance).
3: 19

Say, "O God! Master of Sovereignty! Thou givest sovereignty unto whom Thou wilt, and Thou withdrawest sovereignty from whom Thou wilt. Thou exaltest whom Thou wilt, and Thou abasest whom Thou wilt. In Thy hand is all good. Verily Thou art able to do all things. Thou causest the night to pass into the day, and Thou causest the day to pass into the night. And Thou bringest forth the living from the dead, and Thou bringest forth the dead from the living. And Thou givest sustenance to whom Thou choosest, without measure."
3: 26-27

Ye will not attain unto piety until ye give (freely) of that which ye love; and whatsoever ye give, God is aware thereof.
3: 92

And rush to seek forgiveness from your Lord and for a Paradise as wide as are the heavens and the earth, prepared for the godfearing, those who spend (of that which God hath given them) in (times of) ease and in adversity, those who control their wrath and pardon the offences of their fellow men — for God loveth those who do good — and those who, when they do an evil thing or wrong themselves, remember God and implore forgiveness for their sins — who forgiveth sins save God only? — and will not knowingly repeat (the wrong) they did.
3: 133-135

The life of this world is but the goods and possessions of illusion.
3: 185

O mankind! Be careful of your duty to your Lord who created you from a single soul and from it created its mate and from them twain hath spread abroad a multitude of men and women. Be careful of your duty toward God in whom ye claim (your rights) of one another, and toward the wombs (that bare you). Verily God hath been a watcher over you.
4: 1

Serve God and ascribe no thing as partner unto Him. (Show) kindness unto parents, and unto near kindred, and orphans, and the needy, and unto the neighbor who is of kin (unto you) and the neighbor who is not of kin, and the fellow traveler and the wayfarer and (the slaves) whom your right hands possess. Verily God loveth not such as are proud and boastful.
4: 36

O ye who believe! Stand out firmly for God, as witnesses to fair dealing, and let not hatred of any people seduce you that ye deal not justly. Be just—that is nearer to piety—and fear God. Verily God is well aware of what ye do. God hath promised those who believe and do good works that theirs will be forgiveness and immense reward.
5: 8-9

O ye who believe! Be mindful of your duty to God, and seek the way of approach unto Him, and strive in His way in order that ye may succeed.
5: 35

And there is not an animal in the earth, nor a bird flying on its wings, but they are peoples like unto you. We have neglected nothing in the Book (of our decrees). Then unto their Lord they will be gathered.
6: 38

The Hasht Bihisht (Eight Paradises)
built for Shah Suleiman
Isfahan, Iran

And with Him are the keys of the unseen—none but He knoweth them. And He knoweth whatever is in the land and the sea. Not a leaf falleth but He knoweth it, not a grain amid the darkness of the earth, naught of wet or dry but (it is noted) in a clear record.
6: 59

Leave alone those who take their religion to be mere play and diversion, and are deceived by the life of this world. But proclaim (to them) this (truth): that a soul delivers itself to ruin by its own acts. It will find for itself no protector or intercessor except God.
6: 70

And He it is who hath set for you the stars that ye may guide your course by them amid the darkness of the land and the sea. We have detailed Our signs for people who have knowledge. And He it is who hath produced you from a single being, and (hath given you the earth as) a habitation and a storehouse. We have detailed Our signs for people who have understanding. He it is who sendeth down water from the sky, and therewith We bring forth buds of every kind, and then We bring forth the green leaf from it, from which We bring forth the thick-clustered grain; and from the date-palm, from the pollen thereof, spring pendant bunches; and (We bring forth) gardens of grapes, and the olive and the pomegranate, like each to each, and each unlike to each. Look upon the fruit thereof, when they bear fruit, and upon its ripening. Verily herein are signs for people who believe.
6: 97-100

Forsake all sin, outward or inward; those who earn sin will get due recompense for that which they have earned.
6: 120

Unto your Lord is your return, and He will inform you of that wherein ye used to differ.
6: 164

The Blue Mosque
Istanbul, Turkey

Oasis of Tozeir
Egypt

Call upon your Lord humbly and in secret. Verily He loveth not transgressors. Work not corruption in the earth after the fair ordering thereof, and call on Him in fear and longing. Verily the mercy of God is (always) near to those who do good.
7: 55-56

My mercy embraces all things.
7: 156

And do thou bring thy Lord to remembrance in thy (very) soul, with humility and in awe, without loudness in words, in the mornings and evenings; and be not thou of those who are unheedful.
7: 205

God never changeth the favor He hath bestowed on any people until they first change that which is within themselves.
8: 53

God hath promised to believers, men and women, (heavenly) gardens under which rivers flow, to abide therein forever, and goodly dwelling-places in edenic gardens. But the greatest bliss is the good pleasure of God—that is the supreme felicity.
9: 72

There is no refuge from God save toward Him.
9: 118

To God do belong the unseen (secrets) of the heavens and the earth, and to Him goeth back every affair (for decision). Then serve Him, and put thy trust in Him; and thy Lord is not unmindful of anything that ye do.
11: 123

And He it is who spread out the earth and placed therein firm hills and flowing streams, and in it made all kinds of fruits in pairs. He covereth the night with the day. Verily herein are portents for people who take thought. And in the earth are neighboring tracts, vineyards and ploughed lands, and palms in pairs, and palms single, which are watered with one water. And we have made some of them to excel others in fruit. Surely in that are signs for a people who understand.
13: 3-4

Nay, thunder repeateth His praises, and so do the angels, with awe. He looses the loud-voiced thunder-bolts and smiteth with them whom He will while they dispute (in doubt) concerning God, and He is mighty in wrath. Unto Him is the true prayer. Any others that they call upon besides Him hear them no more than if they were to stretch forth their hands for water to reach their mouths but it reaches them not, for the prayer of those without faith goes only astray. And whosoever is in the heavens and the earth do prostrate themselves to God, willingly or unwillingly, as do their shadows in the mornings and evenings.
13: 13-15

Those who join together those things which God hath commanded to be joined, hold their Lord in awe, and fear the terrible reckoning. Those who patiently persevere in seeking their Lord's countenance and are regular in prayer and give of that which We bestow upon them secretly and openly, and overcome evil with good, for such there is the final attainment of the (heavenly) home. Edenic gardens, they shall enter there, as well as the righteous among their fathers, their spouses, and their offspring, and angels shall enter unto them from every gate (with the salutation), "Peace unto you for that ye persevered in patience! Now how excellent is the (heavenly) home!"
13: 21-24

He guideth to Himself those who turn to Him, those who believe, and whose hearts find satisfaction in the remembrance of God—for without doubt in the remembrance of God do hearts find satisfaction. For those who believe and work righteousness, is (every) blessedness, and a beautiful place of (final) return.
13: 27-29

The Kaaba
Mecca, Saudi Arabia

The Darb-i Iman Mosque
Isfahan, Iran

One day the earth will be changed to other than the earth, as will be the heavens, and they will be marshaled forth, before God, the One, the Irresistible; and thou wilt see the sinners that day bound together in chains ... that God may repay each soul what it hath earned. Verily God is swift at reckoning. Here is a message for mankind that they may take warning therefrom, and let them know that He is (no other than) one God, and let men of understanding take heed.
14: 48-52

For to anything which We have willed, We but say, "Be," and it is.
16: 40

And unto God maketh prostration all that is in the heavens and on earth, whether moving (living) creatures or the angels, and they are not proud.
16: 49

Whoever works righteousness, man or woman, and has faith, verily, to him will We give a new life, a life that is good and pure; and We will bestow on such their reward according to the best of their actions.
16: 97

Thy Lord hath decreed that ye worship none but Him, and that ye be kind to parents. Whether one or both of them attain old age in thy life, say not to them a word of contempt, nor repel them, but address them in terms of honor. And, out of kindness, lower to them the wing of humility, and say, "My Lord! Bestow on them Thy mercy even as they cherished me in childhood." Your Lord knoweth best what is in your hearts. If ye do deeds of righteousness, verily He is most forgiving to those who are penitent. And render to the kindred their due rights, as (also) to those in want, and to the wayfarer; but squander not (your wealth) in the manner of a spendthrift. Verily spendthrifts are brothers of Satan, and Satan is ungrateful to his Lord.... Verily thy Lord doth provide sustenance in abundance for whom He pleaseth, and He provideth in a just measure—for He is aware of and seeth all His servants.... Nor come nigh to adultery, for it is a shameful (deed) and an evil, opening the road (to other evils). Nor

[continued]

[continued]

take life—which God has made sacred—except for just cause.... Come not nigh to the orphan's property except to improve it, until he attains the age of full strength; and fulfill (every) agreement, for (every) agreement will be enquired into (on the Day of Reckoning). Give full measure when ye measure, and weigh with a balance that is straight; that is the most fitting and the most advantageous in the final determination. And pursue not that of which thou hast no knowledge, for every act of hearing, or of seeing, or of (feeling in) the heart will be enquired into (on the Day of Reckoning). Nor walk on the earth with insolence, for thou canst not rend the earth asunder, nor reach the mountains in height. Of all such things the evil is hateful in the sight of thy Lord. These are among the (precepts of) wisdom, which thy Lord has revealed to thee (O Muhammad).
17: 23-39

And restrain thyself with those who call on their Lord morning and evening, seeking His countenance; and let not thine eyes turn away from them, desiring the adornment of the present life. Obey not him whose heart We have permitted to neglect the remembrance of Us, one who follows his own desires, whose case has gone beyond all bounds.
18: 28

Wealth and children are allurements of the life of this world, but the things that endure, good deeds, are better in thy Lord's sight for reward, and better as (the foundation for) hope.
18: 46

Verily those who believe and do good works, theirs are the gardens of Paradise for welcome, wherein they will dwell forever, with no desire to be removed from thence.
18: 107-108

Every soul shall have a taste of death, and We test you with evil and with good by way of trial; and unto Us must ye return.
21: 35

Teouet Kasbah
Meknes, Morocco

Verily, this brotherhood of yours is a single brotherhood and I am your Lord and cherisher, therefore serve Me (and no other).
21: 92

The day that We roll up the heavens like a scroll rolled up for books (completed) — even as We produced the first creation, so shall We produce a new one, a promise We have undertaken. Truly shall We fulfill it.
21: 104

And among mankind is he who worshippeth God upon a narrow margin so that if good befalleth him he is content therewith, but if a trial befalleth him, he falleth away utterly. He loseth both the world and the Hereafter. That is the sheer loss.
22: 11

God is the Light of the heavens and the earth.
24: 35

...Who repenteth and believeth and doth righteous work — as for such, God will change their evil deeds to good deeds. For God is ever-forgiving, most merciful.
25: 70

Do the people think that they will be left alone on saying, "We believe," and that they will not be tested? We did test those before them, and God will certainly know those who are true from those who are false. Do those who practice evil think that they will get the better of Us? Evil is their judgment!
29: 2-4

Journey in the earth and see how He (God) hath brought forth the creation.
29: 20

A Zawiyah in the Old City
Fez, Morocco

Verily worship preserveth from lewdness and iniquity, but verily remembrance (invocation) of God is the greatest (thing in life) without doubt. And God knows the (deeds) that ye do.
29: 45

O... My servants who believe! Truly, spacious is My earth, therefore serve ye Me—(and Me alone)! Every soul shall have a taste of death in the end and to Us shall ye be brought back. But those who believe and work deeds of righteousness, to them shall We give a home in heaven—lofty mansions beneath which flow rivers, to dwell therein secure—an excellent reward for those who do (good), those who persevere in patience, and put their trust in their Lord and cherisher. How many are the creatures that carry not their own sustenance? It is God who feeds (both) them and you, for He hears and knows (all things). If indeed thou ask them who has created the heavens and the earth and subjected the sun and the moon (to their course), they will certainly reply, "God." How are they then deluded away (from the truth)? God enlarges the sustenance (which He gives) to whichever of His servants He pleases; and He (similarly) grants by (strict) measure, (as He pleases), for God has full knowledge of all things. And if indeed thou ask them (creatures and the earth) who it is that sends down rain from the sky, and gives life therewith to the earth after its death, they will certainly reply, "God!" Say, "Praise be to God!" But most of them understand not. What is the life of this world but diversion and play? But verily the abode in the Hereafter—that is life indeed, if they but knew.
29: 56-64

And among His signs are the creation of the heavens and the earth, and the variations in your languages and your colors. Verily in that are signs for those who know. And among His signs are the sleep that ye take by night and by day, and the quest that ye (make for livelihood) out of His bounty; verily in that are signs for those who hearken. And among His signs, He shows you the lightning, by way both of fear and of hope, and He sends down rain from the sky and with it gives life to the earth after it is dead; verily in that are signs for those who are wise. And among His signs is this: that heaven and earth stand by His command; then when He calls you, by a single call, from the earth, behold, ye (straightway) come forth.
30: 22-25

Koran illumination, c. 1363
Cairo, Egypt

School of Tchor Minar
Bukhara, Uzbekistan

And be not of those who ascribe partners (unto Him), those who split up their religion and became schismatics, each sect exulting in its tenets; and when trouble touches them, they cry to their Lord, turning back to Him in repentance; but when He gives them a taste of mercy as from Himself, behold, some of them pay part-worship to other gods besides their Lord, (as if) to show their ingratitude for the (favors) We have bestowed on them! Then enjoy (your brief day); but soon will ye know (your folly).
30: 31-34

Corruption has appeared on land and sea because of (the evil) which men's hands have done, that (God) may give them a taste of some of their deeds, in order that they may turn back (from evil). Say, "Travel through the earth and see what was the end of those before (you). Most of them worshipped others besides God." But set thou thy face to the right religion before there come from God the Day which there is no chance of averting. On that Day shall men be divided (in two). Those who reject faith will suffer from that rejection, and those who work righteousness will spread their couch (of repose) for themselves (in heaven), that He may reward those who believe and work righteous deeds, out of His bounty — for He loves not those who reject faith.
30: 41-45

It is God who sends the winds, and they raise the clouds; then does He spread them in the sky as He wills, and break them into fragments, until thou seest raindrops issue from the midst thereof. Then when He has made them reach such of His servants as He wills, behold, they do rejoice! — even though, before they received (the rain), just before this — they were dumb with despair! Then contemplate (O man) the memorials of God's mercy — how He gives life to the earth after its death. Verily the same will give life to the men who are dead, for He has power over all things.
30: 48-50

Verily those who believe and do good works, for them are the Gardens of Bliss, wherein they will abide. It is a promise of God in truth. He is the All-mighty, the All-wise.
31: 8-9

Establish worship and enjoin the right and forbid the wrong, and persevere whatever may befall thee. Surely this is a bounden duty. And swell
not thy cheek (for pride) at men, nor walk in insolence through the earth;
for God loveth not any arrogant boaster. Be modest in thy bearing and
lower thy voice. Verily the harshest of all voices is the voice of the ass.
31: 17-19

Do ye not see that God has subjected to your (use) all things in the heavens and on earth, and has made His bounties flow to you in exceeding
measure, (both) seen and unseen? Yet there are among men those who
dispute about God, without knowledge and without guidance, and without a Scripture to enlighten them!
31: 20

O mankind! Do your duty to your Lord, and fear (the coming of) a Day
when no father can avail in any way for his son, nor a son avail in any
way for his father. Verily, the promise of God is true; let not then this present life deceive you, nor let the Chief Deceiver (Satan) deceive you about
God. Verily the knowledge of the Hour (of Judgment) is with God (alone).
It is He who sends down rain, and He who knows what is in the wombs.
No soul knoweth what it will earn tomorrow, and no soul knoweth in
what land it will die. Verily God is All-knowing, All-aware.
31: 33-34

For Muslim men and women, for believing men and women, for devout
men and women, for truthful men and women, for men and women who
are patient and constant, for men and women who humble themselves,
for men and women who give in charity, for men and women who fast
(and deny themselves), for men and women who guard their chastity,
and for men and women who engage much in God's praise—for them
has God prepared forgiveness and great reward.
33: 35

O ye who believe, remember God with much remembrance. And glorify
Him morning and evening. He it is who sends blessings on you, as do
His angels, that He may bring you out from the depths of darkness into
light; and He is full of mercy to the believers. Their salutation on the day
(continued)

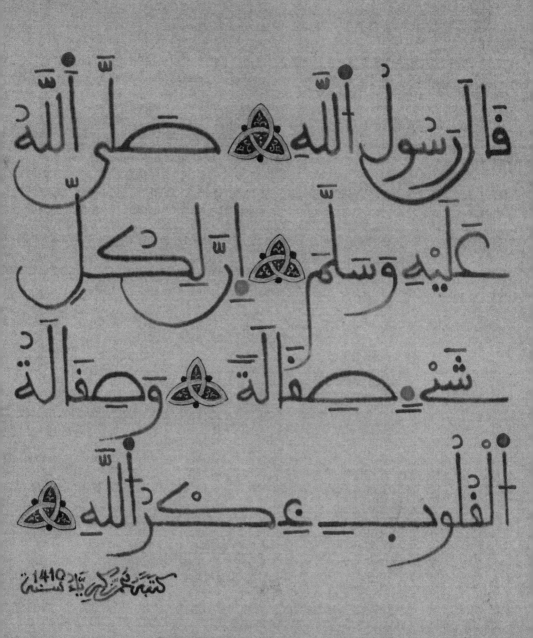

فقال رسول الله صلى الله عليه وسلم إن لكل شيء صقالة وصقالة القلوب ذكر الله

كتبه محمد ... سنة ١٤١٠

Mausoleum of Aba Khoja
Kashgar, China

[continued]

they meet Him will be "Peace!"; and He has prepared for them a generous reward.
33: 41-44

God created you from dust, then from a little fluid, then He made you pairs (the male and female). No female beareth or bringeth forth save with His knowledge; and no one who ageth groweth old, nor has anything taken away of his life, but it is recorded in a Book. Verily that is easy for God.
35: 11

Glory to God, who created in pairs all things that the earth produces, as well as their own (human) kind and (other) things of which they have no knowledge.
36: 36

Assuredly the creation of the heavens and the earth is a greater (matter) than the creation of men, yet most men understand not.
40: 57

Among His signs are the night and the day, and the sun and the moon. Do not prostrate to the sun and the moon, but prostrate to God, who created them, if it is Him ye wish to serve.
41: 37

We shall show them Our signs on the horizons and within themselves until it will be manifest unto them that it is the Truth.
41: 53

For God, He is my Lord and your Lord, so worship ye Him; this is a straight way. But sects from among themselves fell into disagreement; then woe unto those who did evil, from the penalty of a grievous Day!
43: 64-65

God giveth life to you, then causeth you to die, then gathereth you unto the Day of Resurrection whereof there is no doubt; but most of mankind know not
45: 26

To God belongs the dominion of the heavens and the earth, and the day that the Hour of Judgment is established—that day will the dealers in falsehood perish! And thou wilt see every sect bowing the knee. Every sect will be called to its record—this day shall ye be recompensed for all that ye did!
45: 27-28

And verily We shall try you till We know those of you who really strive, and the steadfast, and until We test your record.
47: 31

We verily created man and We know what his soul whispereth to him, and We are nearer to him than his jugular vein.
50: 16

The sun and the moon follow courses (exactly) computed. And the stars and the trees bow in adoration (to Him). And the firmament has He raised high, and He has set up the balance.
55: 5-7

All that dwells upon the earth is perishing, and there remaineth but the countenance of thy Lord of might and glory
55: 26-27

All that is in the heavens and the earth glorifieth God; and He is the All-mighty, the All-wise. To Him belongs the dominion of the heavens and the earth. It is He who gives life and death, and He has power over all things. He is the First and the Last, and the Outward and the Inward; and He is knower of all things. He it is who created the heavens and the earth in six days; then He mounted the Throne. He knoweth all that entereth the earth and all that emergeth therefrom and all that cometh down from the sky and all that ascendeth therein; and He is with you wheresoever ye may be. And God is seer of what ye do.... He causeth the night to pass into the day, and He causeth the day to pass into the night, and He is knower of the secrets of (all) hearts.
57: 1-6

Hasten seeking forgiveness from your Lord.
57: 21

Satan hath engrossed them and so hath caused them to forget remembrance of God.
58: 19

Hasten unto remembrance of God.
62: 9

O ye who believe! Let not your wealth nor your children distract you from remembrance of God; those who do so, they are the losers.
63: 9

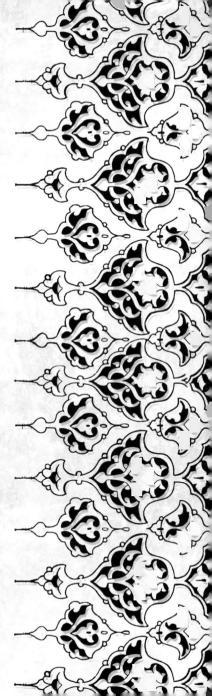

Second Surah of the Koran

He has created the heavens and the earth in just proportions, and has given you shape, and made your shapes beautiful, and to Him is the final goal.
64: 3

God puts no burden on any person beyond what He has given him. After a difficulty, God will soon grant relief.
65: 7

Verily those who fear their Lord in secret, theirs will be forgiveness and a great reward.
67: 12

So obey thou not those who deny (the Truth). They wish that thou shouldst compromise, so that they may compromise.
68: 8-9

Invoke in remembrance the Name of thy Lord, and devote thyself to Him with an utter devotion.
73: 8

And what will convey to thee what the Day of Judgment is? Again, what will convey to thee what the Day of Judgment is? A day when a soul has no control over another, and the sole command that day is God's.
82: 17-19

Surely We created man of the best stature. Then we reduced him to the lowest of the low, save those who believe and do good works, and theirs will be a reward unfailing.
95: 4-6

Rivalry in worldly increase distracteth you until ye visit (your) graves. Nay, but ye will come to know! Nay, but ye will come to know! Nay, would that ye could know with the knowledge of certainty!
102: 1-5

Pilgrimage
sanctuary
Khasvin,
Iran

Verily man is in a state of loss, save those who believe and do good works, and exhort one another to truth and exhort one another to patience and constancy.
103: 2-3

Say: "He, God, is One — God, the Eternal. He begetteth not, nor is He begotten, and there is none equal unto Him."
112: 1-4

Appendix of Additional Koranic Verses

Other Religions
2: 2-4, 2: 106
3: 81, 6: 39
15: 10-11, 16: 43-44
16: 89, 22: 42-53
25: 20, 25: 35-39
37: 108-139, 38: 12-14
43: 6-8, 50: 12-14
51: 38-51, 89: 6-13

The Abrahamic Tradition
Abraham:
2: 124-127
6: 161, 19: 41-50
26: 69-103, 29: 23-29
29: 31, 43: 26-29
Lot:
27: 54-58

Judaism
Moses:
2: 47-67, 2: 92-93
5: 20, 10: 74-93
19: 51-53, 20: 9-99,
21: 48-49, 26: 12-67
27: 7-14, 29: 39-40
32: 23-25, 40: 23-54,
41: 45, 45: 45-48,
46: 12, 61: 5
62: 5

The Children of Israel
3: 93, 5: 12
27: 76-77, 44: 31

Christianity
Jesus:
5: 17, 61: 6
John the Baptist:
3: 38-41

"People of the Book" (Torah, Bible, and Koran)
3: 2-5, 4: 47

Other Messengers from God
Noah:
10: 71-74, 23: 23-30
40: 5, 71: 1-3
Salih and the People of Thamud:
14: 5-13, 27: 45-53

Endnotes

[1] The Koran identifies monasticism in the priesthood as an exaggeration in Christianity. It is important to note that this injunction does not forbid monasticism, but states that God did not ordain or command monasticism for the Christian priesthood. Islam does not separate the sacred and the secular domains, as does monasticism; rather, Islam seeks to bring the essence of monasticism (humility, charity, veracity) into the world (cf. Frithjof Schuon, "The Universality of Monasticism and its Relevance in the Modern World" in *Light on the Ancient Worlds* [World Wisdom, 2006]).

[2] This hadith is often referred to as presenting the essential teachings of Islam, which therefore include believing in all of the sacred scriptures and messengers who were sent by God.

[3] Cf. Koran 21:96.

[4] This is a reference to the covenant that God made with all of the descendents of Adam (Koran 7:172-173).

[5] Cf. Koran 11:80.

[6] This verse of the Koran is shown out of numeric order to balance page lengths.

[7] Cf. Koran 39:68.

[8] "Islam identifies "the Messiah Jesus" as a messenger of God and describes his special status, which is discussed in detail in the Preface; however, the Koran also identifies the concept that God is one of three in a "Trinity" as an exaggeration. A fundamental principle in Islam is the unity of God, thus any idea that relativizes this primordial Unity is considered an exaggeration."

[9] This response is the same greeting that is given to another Muslim.

Glossary of Names and Places

Ad: An ancient tribe that lived after Noah in the village of Aliqaf in Yemen. It was a prosperous tribe, but rebelled against God and their prophet, Hud, and so God destroyed it with a fatal windstorm. Cf. Koran 11:50-60.

Asiya: The wife of Pharaoh. According to a hadith she is one of two perfect women, the other being the Virgin Mary.

Babel: An ancient city in the land of Shinar where the people built the notorious Tower of Babel, which was intended to reach heaven. This is also where the confusion of the language of people took place. Cf. Genesis 11:4-9.

Buraq: The white horse-like animal that Muhammad rode during his ascension to Paradise (*miraj*). Each step of this animal was equal to the range of its vision.

Enoch: An early prophet; Idris in Arabic. Cf. Genesis 5:24; Jude 14; Koran 19:56-57, 21:85.

Gabriel: An archangel, usually appearing as a divine messenger. Cf. Daniel 8:16, 9:21; Luke 1:19, 26; hadith.

Gog and Magog: Two nations led by Satan in a climatic battle at Armageddon. Cf. Revelations 20:8; hadith

Goliath: The giant warrior of the Philistines whom David killed with a stone from a sling. Cf. I Samuel 17:48-51; Koran 2:250-251.

Hadith: A saying of the Prophet Muhammad transmitted outside the Koran through a chain of known intermediaries. There are two kinds of hadith: *hadith qudsi* (sacred sentence), a direct revelation, in which God speaks in the first person by the mouth of the Prophet; and *hadith nabawi* (prophetic sentence), an indirect revelation in which Muhammad speaks in his personal capacity.

GLOSSARY OF NAMES AND PLACES

Haman: The Minister of Pharaoh who tried to have all the newborn babies killed at the time when Moses was born.

Harut: One of the two angels (the other is Marut) that were sent by God as a trial to mankind because God allowed them to teach magic. Cf. Koran 2:102.

Hud: A prophet sent to the Tribe of Ad. Cf. Koran 11:50-60.

Imran: The father of Mary, mother of Jesus. Cf. Koran 3.

Kaaba: The ancient black masonry cube that is the point around which Muslim pilgrims to Mecca make their circumambulations. It is sometimes called the "holy House" in the Koran. It is said to have been originally constructed by Abraham.

Korah: A wealthy man who led a rebellion of 250 men against Moses and Aaron. As a punishment God caused the earth to open and swallow them up along with all that they possessed. Cf. Koran 28:76-82, 29:39.

Magians: Priests of religious settlements from Mesopotamia and its surroundings who existed up to the Christian epoch. They believed in the old nature religion of Iran, which preceded Zoroastrianism. Cf. Koran 22:17.

Manna: Food miraculously supplied to the Israelites in the wilderness. Cf. Exodus 16:15, 16:35; Koran 7:103-170.

Marut: One of the two angels (the other is Harut) that were sent by God as a trial to mankind because God allowed them to teach magic. Cf. Koran 2:102.

Mecca: City in Western Saudi Arabia where Muhammad was born; the spiritual center of Islam.

Medina: City in Western Saudi Arabia where Muhammad was first acknowledged as a messenger from God and where his tomb is located.

Midian: An area in Northwest Arabia near the Gulf of Aqaba named because the people of the region were descended from Midian, a son of Abraham and Keturah. Cf. Genesis 25:1-4; Koran 28:3-43.

Mursaleen: Literally, "those who are sent." It refers both to the prophets and messengers sent by God, whose exact number is not set forth in the Koran or Hadith. Here is a complete list of the prophets and messengers of God who are mentioned in the Koran:

Name of Prophet in Arabic	Approximate Period of Life	Remarks
1. Adam	unknown	The first human
2. Idris	unknown	Enoch
3. Nooh	3900-2900 BC	Noah
4. Hud	2500-2200 BC	Prophet to Ad
5. Salih	2000-1900 BC	Prophet to Thamud
6. Ibrahim	1861-1786 BC	Abraham
7. Lot	1861-1786 BC	Lot
8. Ismael	1781-1638 BC	Ishmael
9. Ishaq	1761-1581 BC	Isaac
10. Yacoub	1700-1653 BC	Jacob
11. Yusuf	1610-1500 BC	Joseph
12. Shuaib	1600-1500 BC	Prophet to Midian
13. Ayoub	1600-1500 BC	Job
14. Musa	1436-1316 BC	Moses
15. Haroon	1439-1317 BC	Aaron
16. Dawood	1043-937 BC	David
17. Sulaiman	985-932 BC	Solomon
18. Dhu'l-Kifel	1600-1500 BC	Ezekiel
19. Ilyas	9th century BC	Elijah
20. Al-Yas	9th century BC	Elisha, successor to Elijah
21. Yunus	8th century BC	Jonah
22. Zakariah	100 BC-20 AD	Zachariah
23. Yahya	1BC-30 AD	John the Baptist
24. Isa	1-33 AD	Jesus
25. Muhammad	571-632 AD	Prophet of Islam

GLOSSARY OF NAMES AND PLACES

Mary: The Virgin Mary, daughter of Imran and Hannah, and mother of Jesus. The Koran says she was chosen above all other women (Cf. Koran 3:42) and the Hadith say that she is one of only two perfect women, the other being Asiya, wife of Pharaoh.

Ar-Rass: One of the villages in the land of Thamud. Cf. Koran 50:12-14, 25:38.

Saabia: The people of Saabia were ruled by the Queen of Sheba. They originally worshipped the stars, moon, and other heavenly bodies until Solomon converted the Queen of Sheba.

Sodom and Gomorrah: Two ancient cities destroyed because of their wickedness. Cf. Genesis 18-19; Koran 15:51-77; hadith.

Thamud: Successors to the people of Ad. They lived in northwestern Arabia between what is now known as Medina and Syria. Their prophet was Salih. God destroyed them with an earthquake. Cf. Koran 7:73-79, 11:61-68, 26:141-159, 27:45-53, 51:43-45, 54:23-31.

Tubba: A village that was destroyed by God because its people did not accept His prophets. Cf. Koran 44:37, 50:14.

Tuwa: The valley of Tuwa on Mount Sinai where Moses conversed with God. Cf. Koran 20:12, 79:16.

Zachariah: The father of John the Baptist and the uncle of the Virgin Mary, who looked after Mary in the Temple of Solomon when she was a temple virgin; in Arabic, Zakariah.

Biographical Notes

Feisal Abdul Rauf is Imam of Masjid al Farah in New York City and founder of the American Sufi Muslim Association (ASMA) Society. He is also a co-founder of the Cordoba Initiative, a multi-faith effort to help heal the relationship between the Muslim world and America. Born in Kuwait to a long line of imams and educated in England, Egypt, and Malaysia, Abdul Rauf is a graduate of Columbia University in New York and holds a master's degree from Stevens Institute of Technology in New Jersey. Abdul Rauf is a member of the board of trustees of the Islamic Center of New York, Islamic advisor to the Interfaith Center of New York, and a board member of One Voice, a group whose initiative is to bring about peace between Israelis and Palestinians. He is also a member of the Council of 100 Leaders to the World Economic Forum on West-Islamic World Dialogue. He is the author of the best selling book, *What's Right With Islam: A New Vision for Muslims and the West*, and often appears in print and broadcast media as an authentic interpreter of Islam.

Judith & Michael Fitzgerald have written and edited numerous publications on world religions. *Christian Spirit* was named "Best Book on Religion & Philosophy" for 2004 by the *Midwest Independent Publisher's Association*. Several of the books they co-edited are used in college classes. Judith is a graduate of Indiana University, an art researcher, and a graphic designer. Three of Michael's books on American Indian spirituality are used in university classes. He has taught Religious Traditions of the North American Indians in the Indiana University Continuing Studies Department at Bloomington, Indiana. He holds a Doctor of Jurisprudence from Indiana University. The Fitzgerald's have spent extended periods of time visiting and photographing traditional cultures and sacred ceremonies throughout the world. They have an adult son and live in Bloomington, Indiana.

What Others Have Said about Michael Fitzgerald:

"He has a great sense of discernment in selecting editorial materials which addresses directly the concerns of the contemporary man."

—Seyyed Hossein Nasr, the George Washington University

"I greatly appreciate the recovery work that Fitzgerald is doing, work that makes available for the classroom and popular use texts that have been all but buried in libraries."

—Stephen Brandon, University of New Mexico

Other Titles from World Wisdom on Islam

Islam, Fundamentalism, and the Betrayal of Tradition:
Essays by Western Muslim Scholars,
edited by Joseph E. B. Lumbard, 2004

The Mystics of Islam,
by Reynold A. Nicholson, 2002

The Path of Muhammad: A Book on Islamic Morals
and Ethics by Imam Birgivi,
interpreted by Shaykh Tosun Bayrak, 2005

Paths to the Heart: Sufism and the Christian East,
edited by James S. Cutsinger, 2003

Paths to Transcendence: According to
Shankara, Ibn Arabi and Meister Eckhart,
by Reza Shah-Kazemi, 2006

The Sufi Doctrine of Rumi: Illustrated Edition,
by William C. Chittick, 2005

Sufism: Love and Wisdom,
edited by Jean-Louis Michon and Roger Gaetani, 2006

Sufism: Veil and Quintessence
A New Translation with Selected Letters,
by Frithjof Schuon, 2007

Tierno Bokar: The Sufi Sage from Mali,
by Amadou Hampaté Ba, translated by Fatima Jane Casewit, 2007

Understanding Islam,
by Frithjof Schuon, 1994

Praise for Other Books in the Sacred Worlds Series:

"One of the great callings of art is to excavate a lost part of our culture, and the Fitzgeralds answer this summons handsomely here in a compact exploration of Native American women's spirituality."
—**Publishers Weekly** on *The Spirit of Indian Women*

"Editors Judith Fitzgerald and Michael Oren Fitzgerald have assembled a fine collection of quotations from Christian saints, writers, and philosophers on the glories and wonders of the natural world. These are accompanied by breathtakingly beautiful photographs of nature."
—**Spirituality & Health** magazine on *The Sermon of All Creation*

"A copy of this beautiful little book should be in every home."
—**Martin Lings**, author of *Muhammad: His Life Based on the Earliest Sources*, on *Christian Spirit*

"*Indian Spirit* is an exceptional book. What strength, dignity and beauty resides in those noble faces! A splendid piece of work by Michael Oren Fitzgerald and World Wisdom."
—**Philip Zaleski**, editor of *The Best Spiritual Writing* series

"This delightful, pocket-sized book lends itself to becoming a companion for the thoughtful religious person on his or her journey through a secular world
—**Hannah Hunt**, Trinity and All Saints College, UK on *Christian Spirit*

"One can get lost in contemplating these photographed faces, the weathered skin of natural men, the dignity which is the outward manifestation of inner strength, patience and wisdom. As for the quotations: [there is] simple grandeur from those who lived on the very face of the earth and the edge of existence."
—**James Alexander Thom**, author of *Follow the River*, *The Long Knife*, and *The Red Heart* on *Indian Spirit*

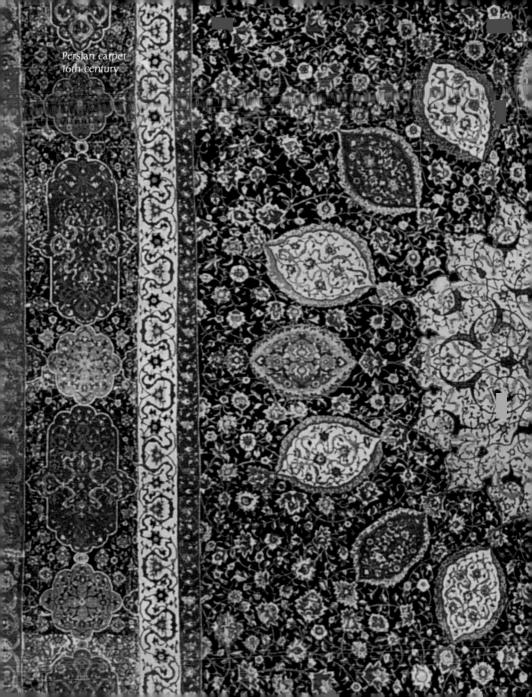

Persian carpet
16th century